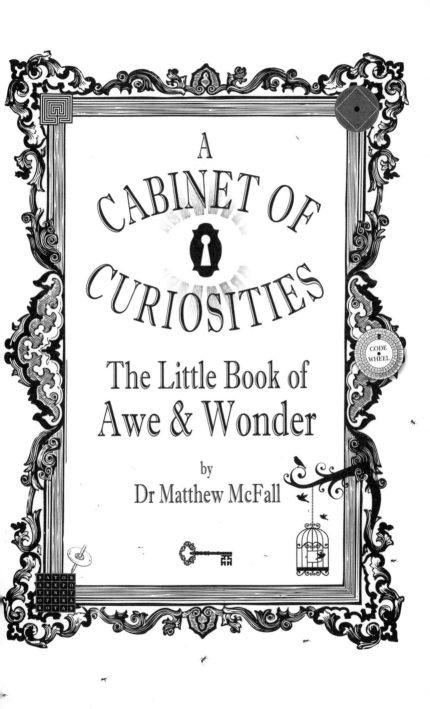

A CABINET OF CURIOSITIES

The Little Book of Awe & Wonder

by
Dr Matthew McFall

A CABINET OF CURIOSITIES

The Little Book of Awe & Wonder

by
Dr Matthew McFall

i Independent Thinking Press

Fertilising Cornucopia (1895) by R. Christiansen

First published by

Independent Thinking Press
Crown Buildings, Bancyfelin, Carmarthen, Wales, SA33 5ND, UK
www.independentthinkingpress.com

Independent Thinking Press is an imprint of Crown House Publishing Ltd.

Image credits can be found on page 243.

British Library Cataloguing-in-Publication Data
A catalogue entry for this book is available
from the British Library.

Print ISBN 978-1-78135-001-0
Mobi ISBN 978-1-78135-012-6
ePub ISBN 978-1-78135-013-3

Printed and bound in the UK by
TJ International, Padstow, Cornwall

FOREWORD

HOW TO SPOT A DESERT ISLAND

Looking is one thing. Noticing is something else entirely. Wanting to notice is what starts it off. It is often remarked that the creative ones are the ones who see what everyone else sees but think something different. Who notice new connections. New patterns. But what makes them want to see the world differently to begin with? Why do they not just walk past the wall at the railway station in the middle of England without noticing the tiny desert island growing there?

Curiosity.

Curiosity is a useful word. It has the same root as the word 'curator'. To look after. To take care. Curiosity is what drives people to want to see the world through a different lens. To notice what's there. And then value what they notice. It is what primes the creative pump. When Einstein was a young boy his father gave him a magnetic compass to play with. He was curious. This curiosity led to him noticing that there was 'something behind things, something deeply hidden'. Curiosity leads to fascination, curiosity's bigger brother (although beware obsession, its evil twin). Curiosity isn't about seeing what isn't there. That's fantasy. It's about taking delight in discovering what is there. Curiosity says, 'I wonder what there is? I wonder what? I wonder ...'

Photograph by Ian Gilbert

i

Wonder.

This is the delight derived from curiosity. Curiosity drives the creative mind. Wonder rewards it. Curiosity motivates us to learn and explore. Wonder is the kickback we get that makes it all worthwhile. S'wonderful.

Wonder is what Matthew McFall does. He has a brain like a museum curator's sock drawer at midnight. Everything is endlessly fascinating. Everything is eminently collectable. Everything is a stimulus for wonder. It's this that he brings to his work in education, entrancing the entire school community, young and old, to want to learn. It's the deliberate process of creating a natural state of wonder that turns learning into the self-satisfying act of satiating one's own curiosity.

This book, for example. It's a wonder. If you are curious enough to explore it you will be amazed at the wonder within it. Wasp hairs. Kidney stone crystals. The lost language of Rongorongo. Divided up into six different compartments, this book is a wonder full of wonders. It's a book to dip in and out of, one in which each page is deliberately there to make you stop. And think. And then see the world differently. 'The only true voyage of discovery, the only fountain of Eternal Youth, would be not to visit strange lands but to possess other eyes', as Proust said. This book shows you how every step you take can be a voyage of discovery. How you'll never be able to look at the world again without wondering. How you'll wonder how you got this far and noticed so little.

It will show you how to make sure you never fail to notice a tiny desert island again.

Ian Gilbert, Suffolk

TO ALL WHO WONDER

A hidden connection is stronger than an obvious one (Heraclitus *Fragments*. c500 BC)

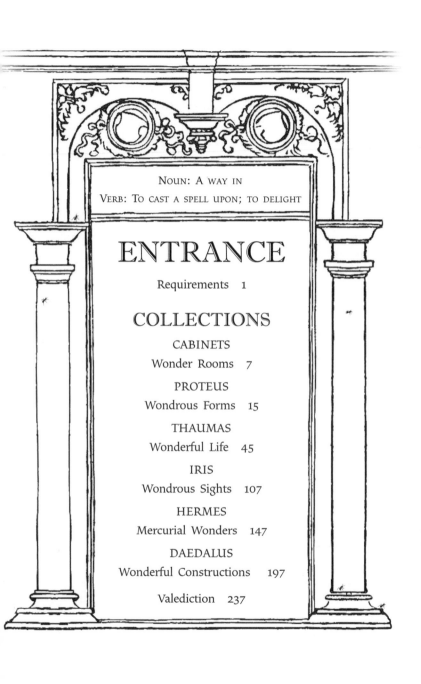

NOUN: A WAY IN
VERB: TO CAST A SPELL UPON; TO DELIGHT

ENTRANCE

$\stackrel{\text{\tiny🔍}}{} = \text{🐜} \times 100$

REQUIREMENTS

Brain v.2013 or earlier.

This book is compatible with all future models.

Optical effects and toys presented here may cause dizziness or nausea if over-explored. Exercise caution.

Your magnifying bookmark will be of great assistance to you.

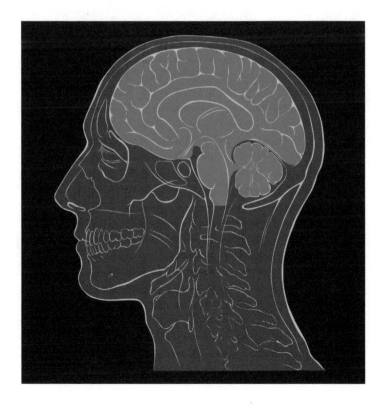

Anatomy of the head, lateral view (Patrick J. Lynch, 2006)

Try to learn something about everything
and everything about something.

Inscription on the memorial stone of Thomas Huxley (1825–1895)

Trompe l'oeil by Cornelis Norbertus Gijsbrechts (fl. 1660–1683)

Curiosity did not kill this cat,
but it did make her smarter.

The Widow (date unknown) by Frederick Dielman (1847–1935)

CURIOSITY ON MARS

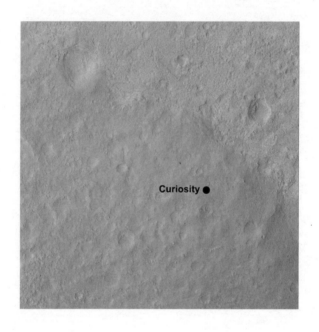

Curiosity ●

Yellowknife Bay, the landing site of NASA's *Curiosity* rover (NASA, 2012)

YOU HAVE A MESSAGE

To access your message you need a pen and paper.

Fold a square of paper four times to produce a grid of sixteen squares as in the example below. Ensure the creases are sharp.

Copy out the message grid below onto your piece of paper.

To read your message:

1. Tear or cut the grid in half from ① to ②. Place the right-hand section on top of the left-hand section (you will be able to see the letters R, Y, E, R, V, U, E, C).

2. Tear through both pieces of paper across the centre from ③ to ④. Place the upper sections on top of the lower sections (you will be able to see the letters R, Y, E, R).

3. Tear through the four sections of paper from ⑤ to ⑥. Place the right-hand sections on top of the left-hand sections (you will be able to see the letters Y and R).

4. Tear through the eight sections of paper from ⑦ to ⑧. Place the upper sections on top of the lower sections. You should have a pack of small pieces with a Y on top.

5. Deal the pieces one at a time in a row from left to right.

6. Your message is now delivered. If you can read it, the message is true.

E	O	① R	⑤ Y ⑦ ⑧
V	Y	E	R ⑥
E	A	③ V	U ④
R	L	E ②	C

'Why,' said the Dodo, 'the best way
to explain it is to do it.'

Lewis Carroll (1832–1898), *Alice's Adventures in Wonderland* (1865)

Illustration by Sir John Tenniel (1820–1914) for the first edition of *Alice in Wonderland*

CABINETS

WONDER ROOMS

RIDDLE

Above us on the cliff the samphire springs,
Salt with the brine of many a stormy night;
Close to the chalk the hornèd poppy clings;
The grey gull shrieks and holds its seaward flight.
And see, low-roofed, where doth to seaward front
My humble First, exposed to tempest's brunt.

Thence starts at break of day the fisher brave,
Launches his skiff, and quickly is afloat
To spread his toils beneath the heaving wave,
And load with finny spoil his little boat:
And aye with curious eye a watch doth keep
Upon my Second's treasures from the deep.

What is it glitters in the dripping mesh?
A ring – perhaps from Caesar's galley lost!
Lost years ago, it visits earth afresh;
Say, what collector would begrudge its cost?
The wealthy antiquary, lucky soul,
Buys it at once to grace my costly Whole.

Riddle by Tom Hood (1835–1874), *Excursions into Puzzledom* (1879)

Answer via code wheel S USTIG – GWB – USTIGWB

CABINETS OF CURIOSITIES

A Cabinet of Curiosities is a room, a display, or a box dedicated to the weird and the wonderful. It is a place for discovery, connection, meaning, and mystery.

The golden age of the Cabinet of Curiosities in Europe was during the sixteenth and seventeenth centuries when large collections could be visited and explored.

It is likely that humans have collected, displayed, studied, and admired interesting objects and artefacts since the dawn of civilization.

A multitude of Cabinets are still in existence, in many different forms.

Illustration from *Wondertooneel der Natuur* Vol. 2 (Levinus Vincent, 1715)

This is the earliest known picture of a Cabinet of Curiosities, from a catalogue of 1599. It depicts Ferrante Imperato's Cabinet in Naples. The man with the stick is thought to be Imperato himself. He appears to pointing at the eye of a crocodile.

Ferrante Imperato (c.1525- c.1615) Dell' Historia Naturale (1599)

This is Oleus Worm's Cabinet in Copenhagen, from his catalogue of 1655. Spot the narwhal's tusk, once thought to be a unicorn horn.

Levinus Vincent (1658–1727) ran a large Cabinet in Haarlem, Holland. The insect displays were reputed to be overwhelming. Vincent also sold fine fabrics. Samples that look like snakes can be seen on a tray in this picture from Vincent's catalogue, *Wonder Theatre of Nature*.

Illustration from *Wondertooneel der Natuur* Vol. 1 (Levinus Vincent. 1715)

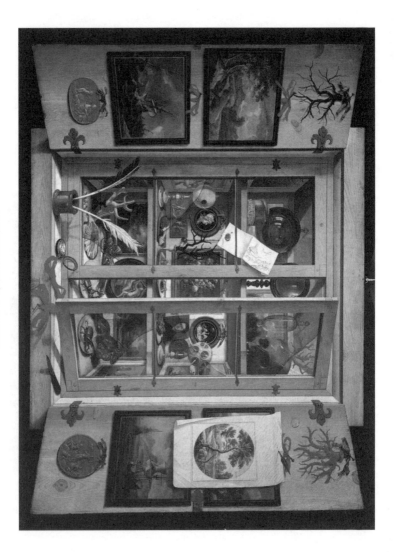

Cabinet of Curiosities (1690) by Domenico Remps

PROTEUS

WONDROUS FORMS

PROTEUS was a shape-shifting god, said to be the oldest son of Poseidon. He lived with a flock of seals on the isle of Pharos. He was reputed to be able to foretell the future, but was very difficult to pin down.

Here the hero Aristaeus is attempting to question Proteus, who is undergoing a terrifying sequence of transformations, including fire, water, snake, spider, and lion.

Aristeus and Proteus (date unknown) by Wenceslas Hollar (1607–1677)

SPOT THE DIFFERENCE

There are five differences between these two pictures. Can you find them?

ON THE SURFACE OF A KIDNEY STONE

Pyramid shaped crystals of weddellite
(calcium oxalate dihydrate).

Scanning electron micrograph (Eugene Karl Kempf, 2012)
Horizontal length of the picture represents 0.5 mm of the original image

Sphinx Mystagoga (1676) by Athanasius Kircher (c.1602–1680)

Fractal growth

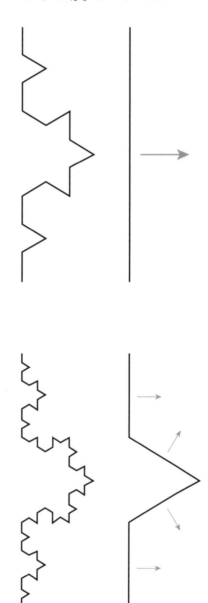

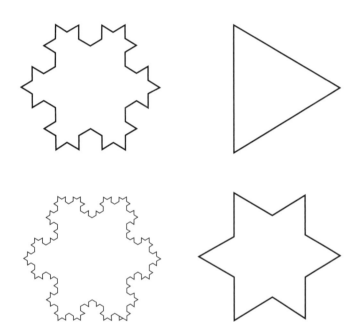

Everything changes and nothing remains still ... and
... you cannot step into the same stream twice.

Heraclitus, 'The Weeping Philosopher' (c535–475 BC)

Nothing exists except atoms and empty space;
everything else is opinion.

Democritus, 'The Laughing Philosopher' (c460–370 BC)

Heraclitus and Democritus (1477) by Donato Bramante (1444–1514)

List of elements (1808) by John Dalton (1766–1844)

Life is a great bundle of little things.

Oliver Wendell Holmes (1809–1894),
The Professor at the Breakfast Table (1859)

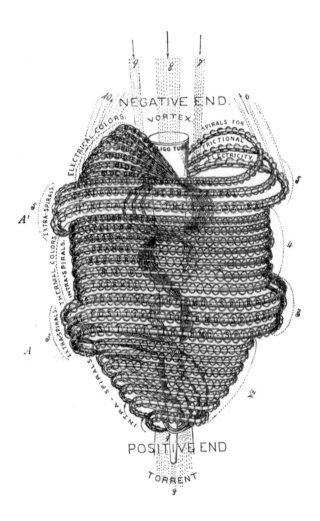

Babbitt's model of the atom from *Principles of Light and Colour* (1878) by Edwin D. Babbitt (1828–1905)

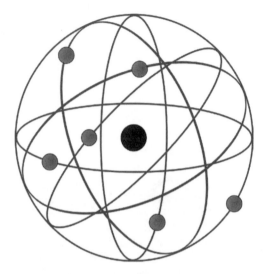

Model of the atom by Ernest Rutherford (1871–1937)

Model of the atom (The World of Wonder 1932)

THIS IS A MODEL OF THE STRUCTURE OF AN ATOM

At the centre is the nucleus, which is understood as a union of protons and neutrons and other elementary particles such as quarks and leptons.

Around the nucleus is an active storm of electrons in orbit.

The electron is the basic unit of electricity.

The word 'electron' comes from the Greek word for amber. Amber, the fossilised gum of trees, when rubbed on fur or certain fabrics, produces sparks of electricity.

Although here they are shown as distinct units, electrons are thought of as smeary clouds which form shells around the nucleus.

Atoms interact with each other via their outermost electrons.

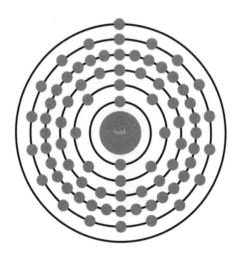

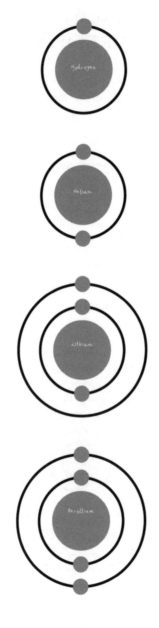

Colour these nuclei and electrons

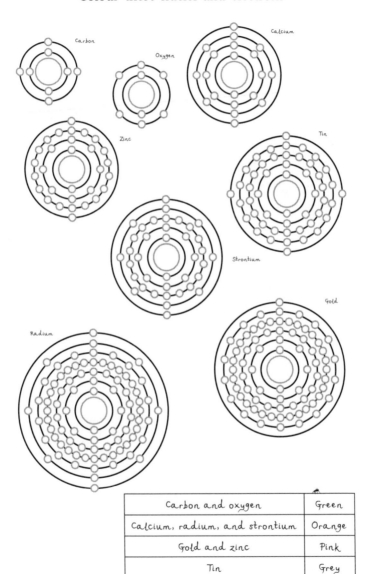

Carbon and oxygen	Green
Calcium, radium, and strontium	Orange
Gold and zinc	Pink
Tin	Grey

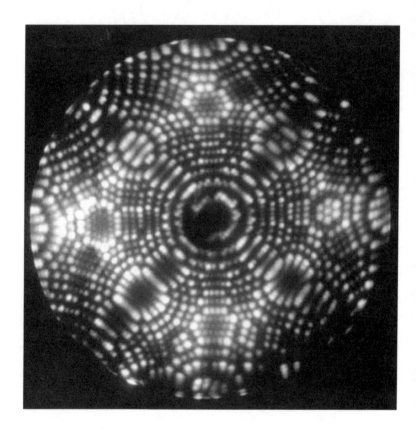

A field ion microscope image of platinum atoms (Tasuo Iwata, 2006).
Each bright spot corresponds to a platinum atom.

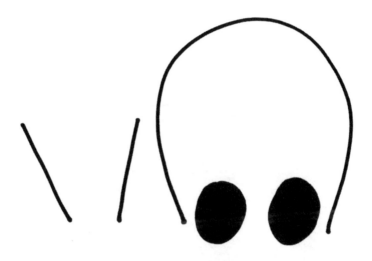

Auntie Mary scrubbing the floor (John Farnsbarns, 2012)

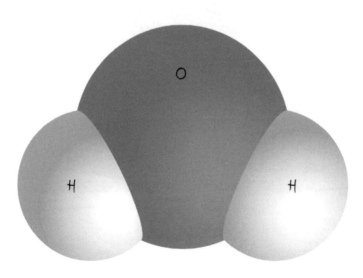

Structure of a water molecule (H_2O) (Solkoll, 2005)

CRYSTALS

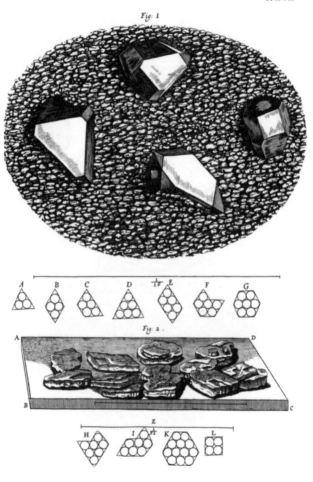

Micrographia (1665) by Robert Hooke (1635–1703)

Protein crystals grown in space (NASA, 2000).
Crystals range in size from a few hundred microns in length up to more than a millimetre

Wilhelm Röntgen discovered X-rays in November 1895. After seeing the first ever X-ray image, a picture of her own hand, Röntgen's wife is reported to have cried: 'I have seen my death!'

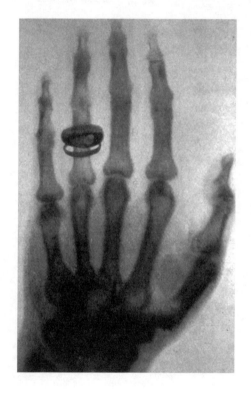

One of the first ever X-ray radiograms (Wilhelm Röntgen, 1845–1923)

Maxwell's discovery of electromagnetic radiation revolutionised the world.

James Clerk Maxwell (1831–1879) holding the colour–matching disc he invented

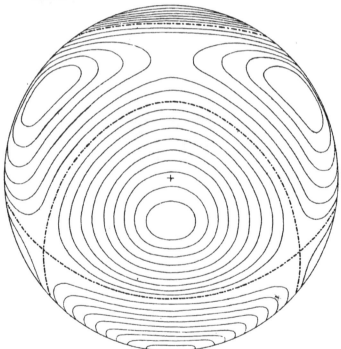

Spherical Harmonic of the third degree.

$$i = 3$$

from *A Treatise on Electricity and Magnetism* (1873)

35

Lissajous figure – a mathematical curve (Solholl, 2005)

HOW SOUNDS ARE MADE VISIBLE TO THE EYE

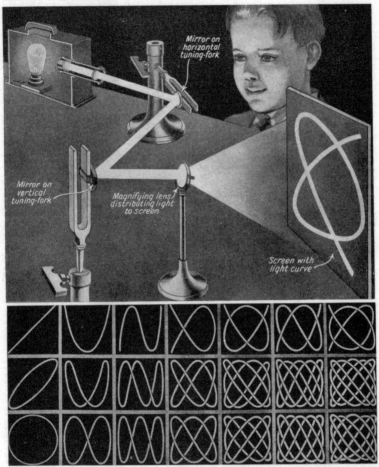

It is possible to make sounds visible to the eye, and the method is shown on this page. In the upper part of the picture we see two tuning-forks to which have been attached small mirrors. One of these forks is placed in a stand horizontally, while the other stands vertically. A powerful beam of light is made to shine into the mirror of the horizontal tuning-fork, and the vertical fork is so placed that the light is reflected into its mirror from the first mirror, and thence passed through a lens so as to shine upon a screen. If now the horizontal tuning-fork be sounded while the second fork remains at rest, the light on the screen becomes a beautiful luminous streak. When the vertical tuning-fork is also sounded in unison with the other, the straight line of light on the screen becomes a bright curve. If, now, a piece of wax be fastened to one of the tuning-forks so that there is a slight difference in its vibration, the luminous figure on the screen will be changed and pass through many variations. When there is a difference of an octave between the tuning-forks the curves on the screen become very complex. The lower part of this picture shows some of the remarkable variations that are presented.

How to Make a Wondergraph

By F. E. TUCK

An exceedingly interesting machine is the so-called wondergraph. It is easy and cheap to make and will furnish both entertainment and instruction for young and old. It is a drawing machine, and the variety of designs it will produce, all symmetrical and ornamental and some wonderfully complicated, is almost without limit. Fig. 1 represents diagrammatically the machine shown in the sketch. This is the easiest to make and gives fully as great a variety of results as any other.

To a piece of wide board or a discarded box bottom, three grooved circular disks are fastened with screws so as to revolve freely about the centers. They may be sawed from pieces of thin board or, better still, three of the plaques so generally used in burntwood work may be bought for about 15 cents. Use the largest one for the revolving table T. G is the guide wheel and D the driver with attached handle. Secure a piece of a 36-in. ruler, which can be obtained from any furniture dealer, and nail a small block, about 1 in. thick, to one end and drill a hole through both the ruler and the block, and pivot them by means of a wooden peg to the face of the guide wheel. A fountain pen, or pencil, is placed at P and held securely by rubber bands in

part way into its upper edge. Any one of these nails may be used to hold the other end of the ruler in position, as shown in the sketch. If the wheels are not true, a belt tightener, B, may be attached and held against the belt by a spring or rubber band.

After the apparatus is adjusted so it will run smoothly, fasten a piece of drawing paper to the table with a couple of thumb tacks, adjust the pen so that it rests lightly on the paper and turn the drive wheel. The results will be surprising and delightful. The accompanying designs were made with a very crude combination of pulleys and belts, such as described.

The machine should have a speed that will cause the pen to move over the paper at the same rate as in ordinary writing. The ink should flow freely from the pen as it passes over the paper. A very fine pen may be necessary to prevent the lines from running together.

The dimensions of the wondergraph may vary. The larger designs in the illustration were made on a table, 8 in. in diameter, which was driven by a guide wheel, 6 in. in diameter. The size of the driver has no effect on the form or dimensions of the design, but a change in almost any other part of

An Easily Made Wondergraph

a grooved block attached to the ruler. A strip of wood, MN, is fastened to one end of the board. This strip is made just high enough to keep the ruler parallel with the face of the table, and a row of small nails are driven

the machine has a marked effect on the results obtained. If the penholder is made so that it may be fastened at various positions along the ruler, and the guide wheel has holes drilled through it at different distances from the center

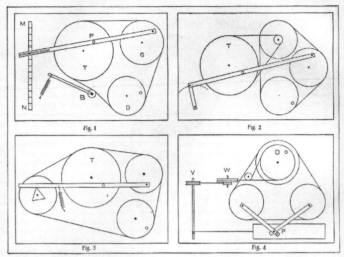

Diagrams Showing Construction of Wondergraphs

to hold the peg attaching the ruler, these two adjustments, together with the one for changing the other end of the ruler by the rows of nails, will make a very great number of combinations possible. Even a slight change will greatly modify a figure or give an entirely new one. Designs may be changed by simply twisting the belt, thus reversing the direction of the table.

If an arm be fastened to the ruler at right angles to it, containing three or four grooves to hold the pen, still different figures will be obtained. A novel effect is made by fastening two pens to this arm at the same time, one filled with red ink and the other with black ink. The designs will be quite dissimilar and may be one traced over the other or one within the other according to the relative position of the pens.

Again change the size of the guide wheel and note the effect. If the diameter of the table is a multiple of that of the guide wheel, a complete figure of few lobes will result as shown by the one design in the lower right-hand corner of the illustration. With

a very flexible belt tightener an elliptical guide wheel may be used. The axis may be taken at one of the foci or at the intersection of the axis of the ellipse.

The most complicated adjustment is to mount the table on the face of another disc, table and disc revolving in opposite directions. It will go through a long series of changes without completing any figure and then will repeat itself. The diameters may be made to vary from the fraction of an inch to as large a diameter as the size of the table permits. The designs given here were originally traced on drawing paper 6 in. square.

Remarkable and complex as are the curves produced in this manner, yet they are but the results obtained by combining simultaneously two simple motions as may be shown in the following manner: Hold the table stationary and the pen will trace an oval. But if the guide wheel is secured in a fixed position and the table is revolved a circle will be the result.

So much for the machine shown in

438

Specimen Scrolls Made on the Wondergraph

Fig. 1. The number of the modifications of this simple contrivance is limited only by the ingenuity of the maker. Fig. 2 speaks for itself. One end of the ruler is fastened in such a way as to have a to-and-fro motion over the arc of a circle and the speed of the table is geared down by the addition of another wheel with a small pulley attached. This will give many new designs. In Fig. 3 the end of the ruler is held by a rubber band against the edge of a thin triangular piece of wood which is attached to the face of the fourth wheel. By substituting other plain figures for the triangle, or outlining them with small finishing nails, many curious modifications such as are shown by the two smallest designs in the illustrations may be obtained. It is necessary, if symmetrical designs are to be made, that the fourth wheel and the guide wheel have the same diameter.

In Fig. 4, V and W are vertical wheels which may be successfully connected with the double horizontal drive wheel if the pulley between the two has a wide flange and is set at the proper angle. A long strip of paper is given a uniform rectilinear motion as the string attached to it is wound around the axle, V. The pen, P, has a motion compounded of two simultaneous motions at right angles to each other given by the two guide wheels. Designs such as shown as a border at the top and bottom of the illustration are obtained in this way. If the vertical wheels are disconnected and the paper fastened in place the well known Lissajou's curves are obtained. These curves may be traced by various methods, but this arrangement is about the simplest of them all. The design in this case will change as the ratio of the diameters of the two guide wheels are changed.

These are only a few of the many adjustments that are possible.

The Boy Mechanic (1913) (H. H. Windsor)

40

Jules Lissajous (1822–1880)
French mathematician and inventor of the Lissajous apparatus, forerunner of the Wondergraph.

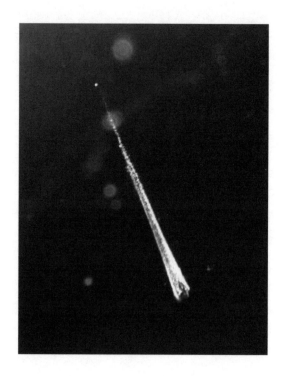

Stardust fragment caught in aerogel (NASA, 2006)

This quiet Dust was Gentlemen and Ladies
And Lads and Girls —
Was Laughter and Ability and Sighing
And Frocks and Curls.

'This Quiet Dust' (c.1864), Emily Dickinson (1830–1886)

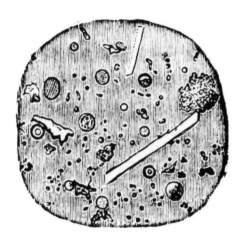

Corpuscles of dust (*Popular Science Monthly*, 1876)

THAUMAS

WONDERFUL LIFE

'What an Aquarium Should Be' (*Illustrated Sporting and Dramatic News*, 1876)

THAUMAS

The Greek god, whose name means WONDER,
is the child of Earth and Sea.

He is the father of Iris, the Rainbow,
and the Harpies, whom some say are beautiful
and some say are hideous.

... from so simple a beginning endless forms
most beautiful and most wonderful have been,
and are being, evolved.

Charles Darwin (1809–1882), *On the Origin of Species* (1859)

Selection of Shells Arranged on Shelves (early 19th century) by Alexandre Isidore Leroy de Barde (1777–1828)
(C) RMN–Grand Palais (musée du Louvre)

Water (1566) by Giuseppe Arcimboldo (1527-1593)

Bathykorus bouilloni (US Oceanic and Atmospheric Administration, 2005)

Everything has its beauty, but not everybody sees it.

Confucius (c550–c478 BC), Analects

Photograph of giant squid in bath tub, Logy Bay, Newfoundland (1873)

J. HOLLOWAY
Rostrevor House

32, Cambray Place
CHELTENHAM.

Mrs Gren? (no date), author's collection

LIVING THINGS EXHIBIT THESE SIGNS OF LIFE, MOST OF THE TIME:

Movement

Respiration

Sensitivity

Growth

Reproduction

Excretion

Nutrition

History tells us that this sequence was first identified by Mrs Gren, goodness-knows-when, whose name lives on in a cunning acronym. Read the first letter of each word in the list of the signs of life.

What was Mrs Gren's first name? We will never know. Make one up by devising your own acronym of qualities, e.g.

ELSIE

Enthusiasm

Listlessness

Serendipity

Intelligence

Empathy

Is ditchwater dull? Naturalists with microscopes
have told me that it teams with quiet fun.

G. K. Chesterton (1874–1936), *The Spice of Life* (1936)

There are more than 100,000 living species of diatom. You can
collect diatoms from a muddy puddle, but will need a
microscope to see them.

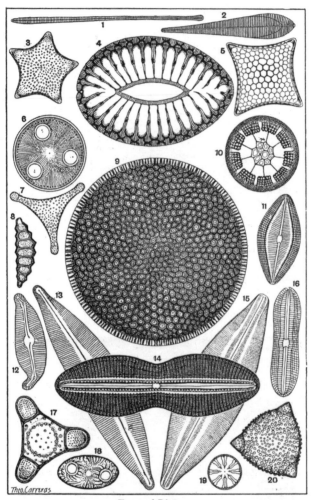

Types of Diatoms.

1. Licmophora flabellata. 2. Licmophora Ehrenbergii. 3. Triceratium punctatum var. penta-gona. 4. Surirella sentis. 5. Triceratium quadrata. 6. Auliscus normanianus. 7. Triceratium arietinum. 8. Eunotogramma variabile. 9. Coscinodiscus robustus. 10. Asterolampra insignis. 11. Navicula nitescens. 12. Encyonema prostratum. 13. Cymbella heteropleura. 14. Navicula pandura. 15. Navicula lyra var. recta. 16. Navicula gemmata. 17. Triceratium sulcum. 18. Auliscus ovalis. 19. Actinoptychus tener. 20. Triceratium turgidum. (All Figs. from Schmidt, except *Licmophoræ*, which are from Henrek.)

The Harmsworth Encyclopedia: Everybody's Book of Reference (c.1905)

55

Diatomea from Kunstformen der Natur (1904) by Ernst Haeckel (1834–1919)

AN ENLIGHTENMENT OF COLLECTIVE NOUNS

A school of fish

A charm of finches

A whoop of gorillas

A smack of jellyfish

A knot of toads

A clowder of cats

A peep of chickens

A skulk of foxes

A game of swans

A parliament of owls

A labour of moles

A dray of squirrels

A murder of crows

An exaltation of larks

An unkindness of ravens

A clew of worms

A walk of snails

A mess of iguanas

Everything is from an egg. (Ex ovo omnia).

William Harvey (1578–1657), *Exercitationes de Generatione Animalium* (1651)

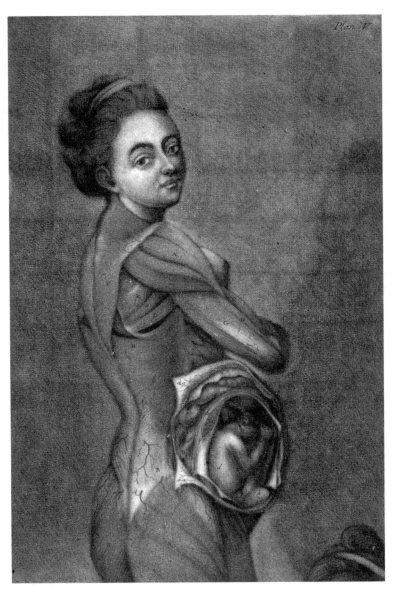

Anatomy of a Pregnant Woman (1773) by Jacques Fabien Gautier D'Agoty (1716-1785)

1. European Honey Buzzard
2. Falcon
3. Eurasian Sparrow-Hawk
4. Blackbird
5. Thrush
6. Rook
7. Corn Bunting
8. Grosbeak
9. Sparrow
10. Chaffinch
11. Pipit
12. Reed Bunting
13. Cuckoo
14. Hummingird
15. Crossbill
16. Wren
17. Nuthatch
18. Nightingale
19. Goldcrest
20. Accentor
21. Rock Bunting
22. Reed Warbler
23. Sedge Warbler
24. Warbler
25. Tit
26. Tree Warbler
27. Waxwing
28. Oriole
29. Jacana
30. Grouse
31. Grouse
32. Pheasant
33. Partridge
34. Quail
35. Avocet
36. Spotted Redshank
37. Dotterel
38. Plover
39. Lapwing
40. Green Sandpiper
41. Tern
42. Common Tern
43. Tern
44. Seagull
45. Loon
46. Guillemot
47. Great Auk
48. Puffin
49. Puffin
50. Grebe
51. Pond Turtle
52. Land Tortoise
53. Dogfish
54. Dogfish
55. Shark
56. Chimaera
57. Lamprey
58. Cuttlefish
59. Tiger Moth
60. Geometer Moth
61. Geometer Moth
62. Clouded Yellow Butterfly
63. Figure of Eight Moth
64. Wall Butterfly
65. Skipper Butterfly
66. Noctuid Moth
67. Buff Moth
68. *Ennemos* Moth
69. Atlas Moth
70. Admiral Butterfly
71. *Bryophila* Moth
72. *Catarhoe* Moth

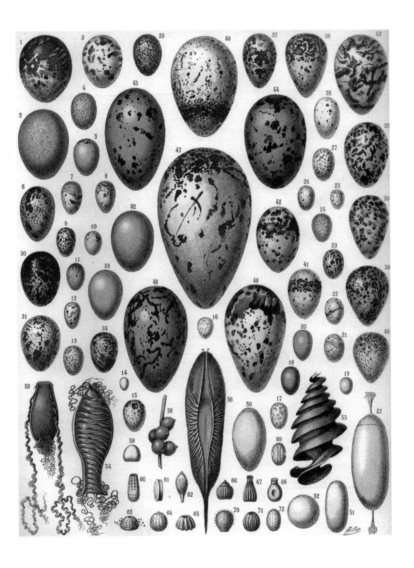

Oeufs from *Nouveau Larousse Illustré, Vol. 6* by Adolphe Millot (1857-1921)

A hen is only an egg's way of making another egg.

Samuel Butler (1835–1902), *Life and Habit* (1877)

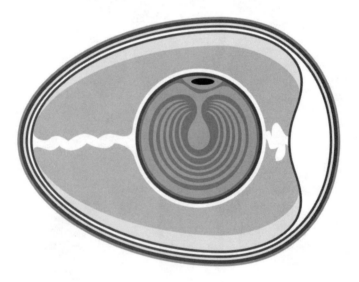

Anatomy of an egg (Horst Frank, 2008)

This is a parasite that lives in the alimentary
canal of molluscs and fish.

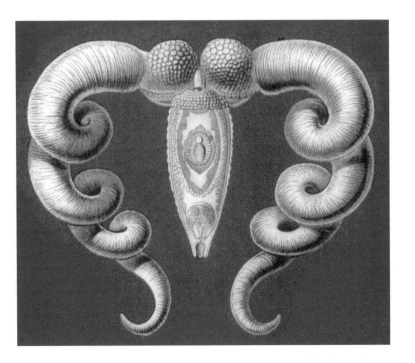

The larva of the ox head flatworm from *Kunstformen der Natur* (1904) by Ernst Haeckel (1834–1919)

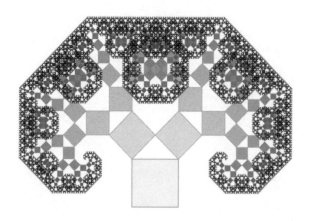

Pythagoras tree (Guillaume Jacquernot, 2010)

LICHEN

Lichen can be found all around you, if you know where to look.

They can be seen in the city, town, and countryside, growing on pavements, walls, roofs, and trees.

They are easy to overlook and can be found in many unexpected places.

The folk name for lichen is TIME STAIN.

Lichens from *Kunstformen der Natur* (1904) Ernst Haeckel (1834–1919)

All my life through, the new sights of nature
made me rejoice like a child.

Marie Curie (1867–1934)

Glaucus lineatus (1868) by Rudolph Bergh (1824–1909)

Phaeodaria from Kunstformen der Natur (1904) by Ernst Haeckel (1834–1919)

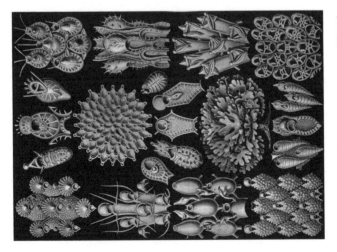

Bryozoa from Kunstformen der Natur (1904) by Ernst Haeckel (1834–1919)

Ophiodea, from *Kunstformen der Natur* (1904) by Ernst Haeckel (1834–1919)

Amphoridea, from *Kunstformen der Natur* (1904) by Ernst Haeckel (1834–1919)

Cirripedia, from *Kunstformen der Natur* (1904) by Ernst Haeckel (1834–1919)

Spirobrachia, from *Kunstformen der Natur* (1904) by Ernst Haeckel (1834–1919)

The Crab and its Mother (1668) by Wenceslas Hollar (1607–1677)

A mother crab, watching her child, said:
'Walk properly. Pick yourself up, walk straight, and don't drag your bottom on the sand.'
The young crab replied:
'Mother, teach me how. Show me first and I will learn from you.'

Moral: Teach by example and learn by example.

Aesop (c.6th century BC), translated J. M. Pilfold

Japanese spider crab (*Popular Science Magazine*, 1920)

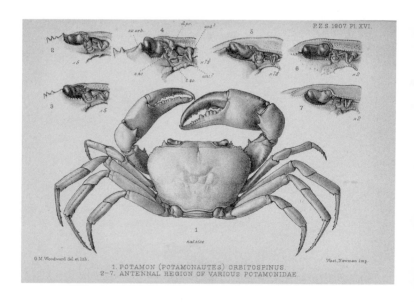

P.Z.S. 1907 Pl. XVI.

G.M. Woodward del. et lith.

West, Newman imp.

1. POTAMON (POTAMONAUTES) ORBITOSPINUS.
2–7. ANTENNAL REGION OF VARIOUS POTAMONIDAE.

Crabs' eyes (Proceedings of the Zoological Society, 1907)

A Poodle (1649) by Wenceslas Hollar (1607–1677)

Great fleas have little fleas upon
their backs to bite 'em,
And little fleas have lesser fleas, and so *ad infinitum.*

Augustus de Morgan (1806–1871), *A Budget of Paradoxes* (1872)

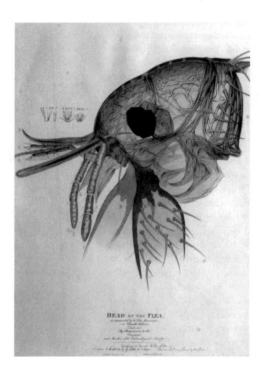

'Head of the Flea' by William Lens Aldous (1792–1878) (*Entomological Society of London, c.*1838)

EAR MITE

This is a magnified view of *Otodectes,* an arachnid that lives in the wax of the ears of dogs and humans.

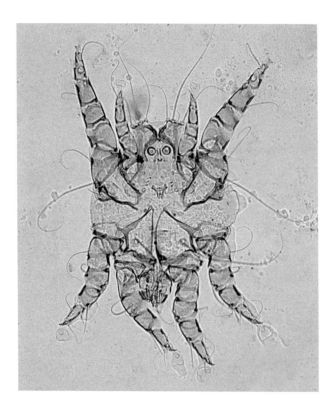

Otodectes ear mite (Alan Walker, 2012)

BEETLE ANTENNAE

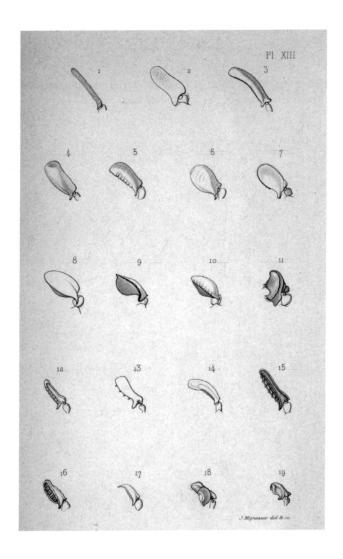

Beetle antennae from the *Descriptive Catalogue of the Coleoptera of South Africa* (1897) by Louis Péringuey (1855–1924)

This is something you may have seen but magnified here many times – what is it?

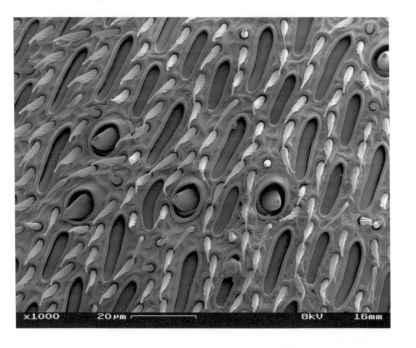

Vespula vulgaris under a scanning electron microscope
The scale bar represents 20 μm (magnification 1000x) (Secret Disc, 2007)

A wasp's antenna.

Face of a southern yellow jacket queen. (Vespula squamosa) (Oyo Threter, 2009)

If you wish to live and thrive, let a spider run alive.

Folk wisdom

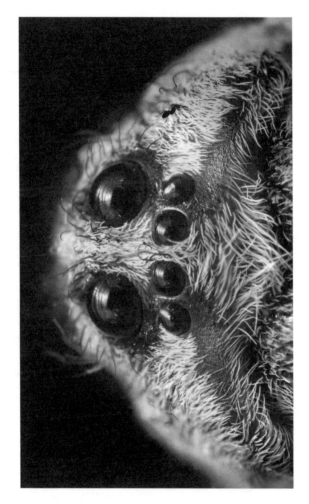

Face of a wolf spider (Opo Terser, 2008)

The bite of the tarantula was once thought curable by dancing to the music of the tarantella.

(Tarantella is Italian for tarantula.)

Here the great wonderer Athanius Kircher provides a tune used in southern Italy, along with a helpful map and identification guide.

Warning: if you are bitten by a tarantula, the tarantella is unlikely to make you better

From Magnes, sive de arte magnetica opus tripartitum (1641) by Athanasius Kircher (c.1601–1680)

Dissection of spider, showing stomach and part of the alimentary canal (left) and heart and arteries (right).

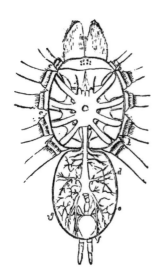 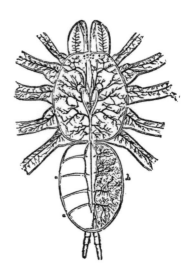

Mygale blondii

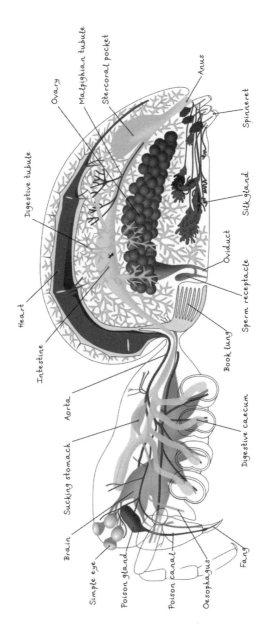

Internal anatomy of the female two-lunged spider from *The Spider Book* (1912) by John Henry Comstock (1849-1931)

Face of a wolf spider (Thomas Shahan, 2010)

This is a strange and tricky riddle, over 500 years old.

Three prisoners such as it was,
Were shut up in a prison of glass.
The prison door was made of bread,
And yet they were from hunger dead.

What does it describe?

This describes how someone caught three flies in a glass and prevented their
escape by placing a slice of bread over the mouth of the glass

Q: WHAT IS THE MOST COMPLEX THING IN THE KNOWN UNIVERSE?

A: The brain you are using to read this.

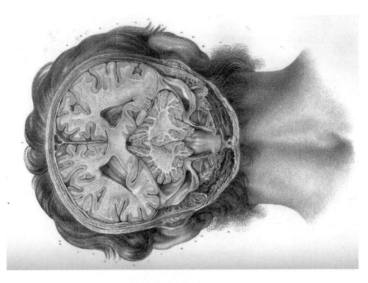

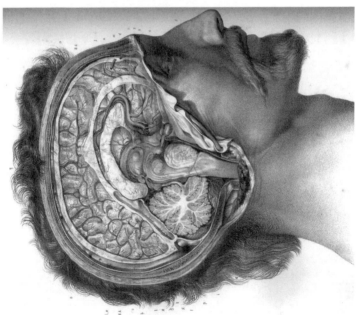

From Traité complet de l'anatomie de l'homme (1862) by Nicolas-Henri Jacob (1782–1871) and Jean-Baptiste Bourgery (1797–1849)

What has eyes but cannot see?
What has arms but no hands?
What has a face but no eyes?
What has a chest but no shoulders?
What has hands but no arms?
What has palms but no wrists?
What has a heart but no kidneys?
What has wings but no legs?
What has a tongue but no mouth?
What has nails but no hands or feet?

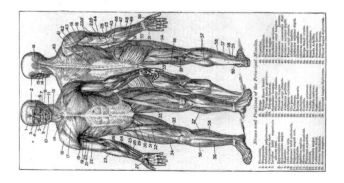

Muscles (The Harmsworth Encyclopedia. Everybody's
Book of Reference. (c.1905)

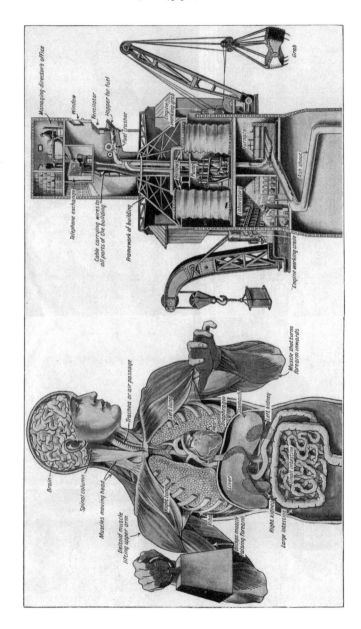

Human compared to a factory (The World of Wonder, 1933)

THE ALIMENTARY CANAL

The alimentary canal or digestive tract is a long tube of different types of flesh.

It begins at the mouth and ends at the anus and in an adult human is approximately 9 metres long.

'Alimentary' comes from the Latin word *alimentare*, nourish.

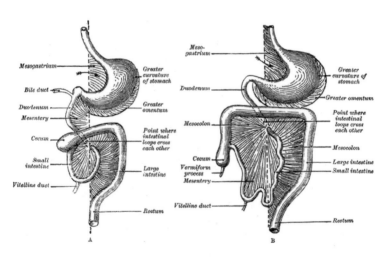

From Gray's Anatomy of the Human Body (1918) by Henry Gray (1827–1861)

SPLANCHNOLOGY:
The study of the viscera or entrails.

It's a very odd thing –
As odd as odd can be –
That whatever Miss T eats
Turns into Miss T.

'Miss T' (1913), Walter de la Mare (1873–1956)

'Eat Your Soup' A baby and his from a French catalogue c.1890

THE STOMACH

The stomach is a bag of muscle that secretes acid, enzymes, and mucous, killing bacteria and dissolving food so that it can be absorbed by the body on its journey through the alimentary canal.

In humans, the stomach is usually found in the thorax, just below the heart.

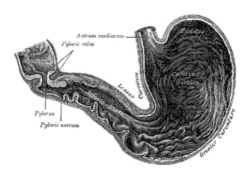

From Gray's Anatomy of the Human Body (1918) by Henry Gray (1827–1861)

Filling Your Stomach

From Gray's Anatomy of the Human Body (1918) by Henry Gray (1827–1861)

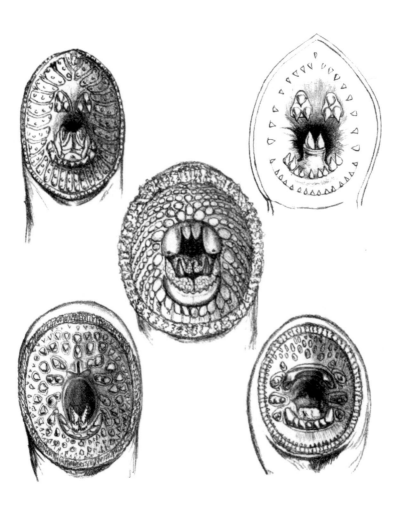

The mouths of lampreys (*Proceedings of the Zoological Society of London,* 1851)

Radula (snail teeth), magnification 130x (*Smithsonian Contributions to Zoology*, 1979)

LOVE DARTS

As part of their reproductive behaviour, some slugs and snails (gastropods) spear one another with darts they fire from their heads.

Love darts are also known as gypsobela.

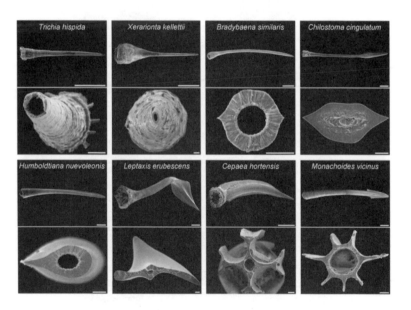

Scanning electron micrograph images of assorted love darts from Joris M. Koene and Hinrich Schulenberg, 'Shooting darts: co-evolution and counter-adaptation in hermaphroditic snails' (BMC *Evolutionary Biology*, 2005). The upper images are love darts from the side, with a scale bar of 500 µm (0.5 mm). The lower images are cross-sections, with a scale bar of 50 µm (0.05 mm)

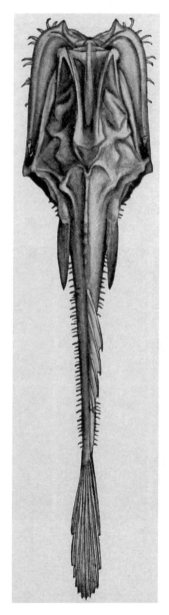

Thaumatichthys (Proceedings of the United States National Museum, 1917)

Anglerfish, also known as the monkfish. *Lophius piscatorius* (*Popular Science Monthly*, 1879)

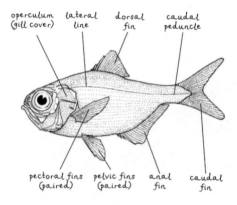

operculum
(gill cover)

lateral
line

dorsal
fin

caudal
peduncle

pectoral fins
(paired)

pelvic fins
(paired)

anal
fin

caudal
fin

Anatomy of a splendid alfonsino from *Collins Guide to the Sea Fishes of New Zealand*, by Tony Ayling and Geoffrey Cox (1982)

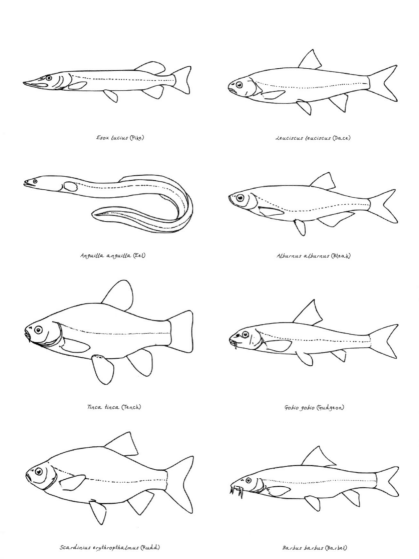

Esox lucius (Pike)

Leuciscus leuciscus (Dace)

Anguilla anguilla (Eel)

Alburnus alburnus (Bleak)

Tinca tinca (Tench)

Gobio gobio (Gudgeon)

Scardinius erythrophthalmus (Rudd)

Barbus barbus (Barbel)

From 'Mammalia, Aves, Reptilia, Amphibia, Pisces' (1909) by P. Matschie, A. Reichenow, G. Tornier and P. Pappenheim
in A. Brauer, *Die Süsswasserfauna Deutschlands*

Big Fish Eat Little Fish (1556) by Pieter Breugel the Elder (c.1526/1530–1569)

Hydra from *Locapletissimi Rerum Naturalium Thesauri*, Vol. 1 (1734) by Albertus Seba (1665–1736)

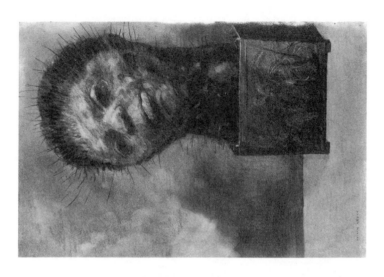

Cactus Man (1881) by Odilon Redon (1840-1916)

Portrait of Young Woman with Unicorn (c.1505) by Raphael (1483-1520)

Centipede (Popular Natural History, 1925)

While strange creepy creatures
came out of their dens,

And watched them with wondering eyes.

Lewis Carroll (1832–1898). The Hunting of the Snark (1874)

Illustration by Henry Holiday (1839–1927) for The Hunting of the Snark (1876)

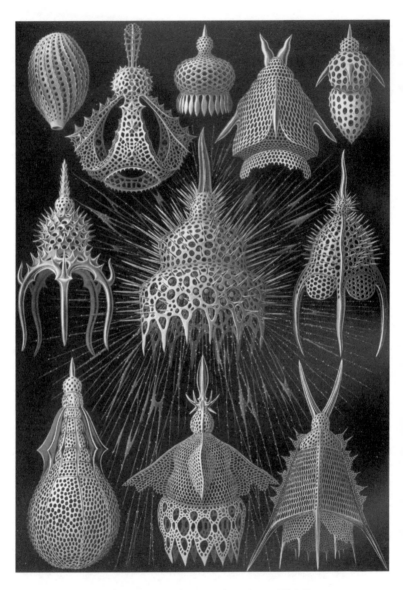

Cyrtoidea from Kunstformen der Natur (1904) by Ernst Haeckel (1834–1919)

In its mysterious past, it encompasses all the
dim origins of life and receives in the end ... the
dead husks of that same life. For all at last
return to the sea – to Oceanus, the ocean river,
like the ever-flowing stream of time, the
beginning and the end.

Rachel Carson (1907–1964), *The Sea around Us* (1951)

IRIS

WONDROUS SIGHTS

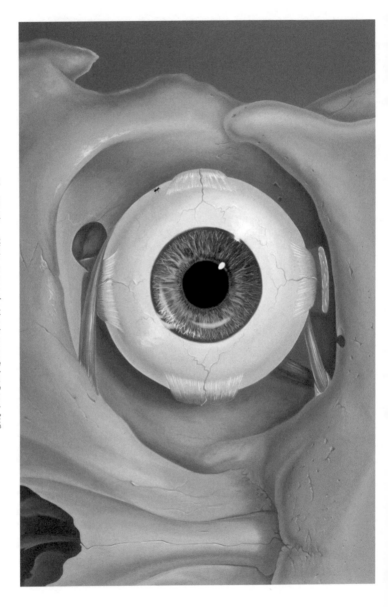

Normal anatomy of the human eye and orbit, anterior view (Patrick J. Lynch, 2006)

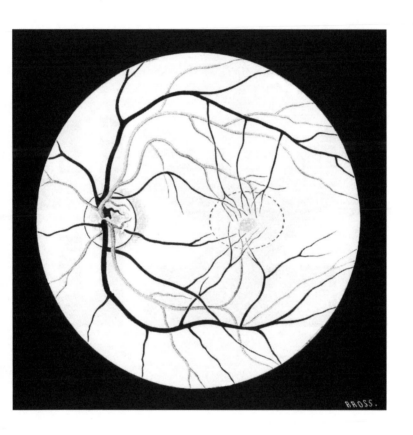

Visual portion of the retina as seen by ophthalmoscope (*Popular Science Monthly*, 1894)

PYO UREY ESOPE NFORW ONDERF ULTHINGS

Iris missouriensis from *An Illustrated Flora of the Northern United States, Canada and the British Possessions* by Nathaniel Lord Britton and Addison Brown (1913)

Starlet (*The World of Wonder* 1933)

In Greek mythology, IRIS is the daughter of Wonder (Thaumas).

She is the goddess of the rainbow and, like Hermes, a messenger of the gods.

Engraving of Iris by Thomas Piroli (1752–1824) from John Flaxman's *Iliad of Homer* (1795)

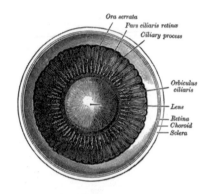

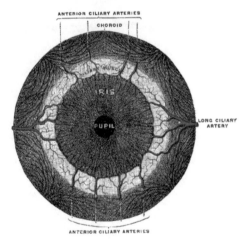

Eyelash mite Demodex folliculorum (Popular Science Monthly, 1878–1879)

From Gray's Anatomy of the Human Body (1918) by Henry Gray (1827–1861)

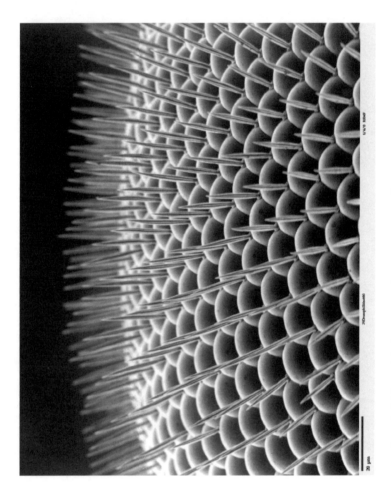

The eye of a fruit fly magnified under a scanning electron microscope (Louisa Howard, 2008). Scale bar (bottom left corner) is 20 μm.

Find Your Blind Spot

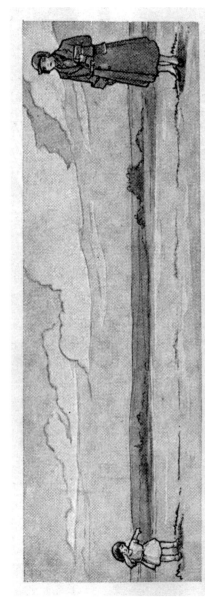

Close your left eye and holding the page about two feet away look at the child. The mother will also be visible. Now bring the page slowly nearer to your face and at one point the mother will disappear altogether

The wonder of the blind spot in the eye (The World of Wonder, 1935)

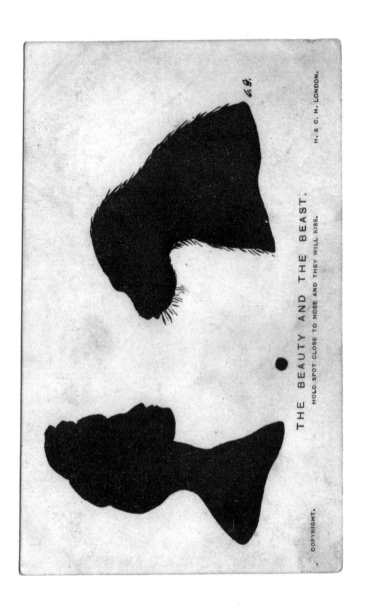

Postcard by H & C H London (no date) author's collection

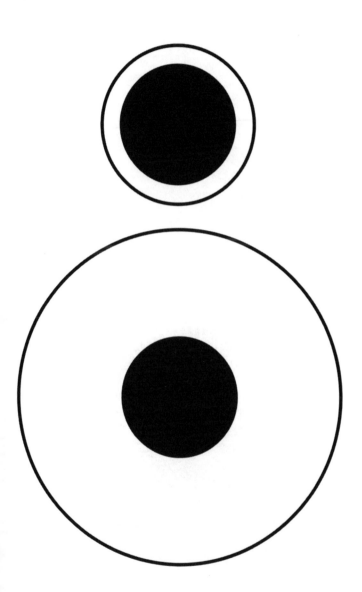

The Delboeuf illusion: both black circles are the same size

A star with 1024 points (Mifter, 2008)

A star with 100 points (Mifter, 2008)

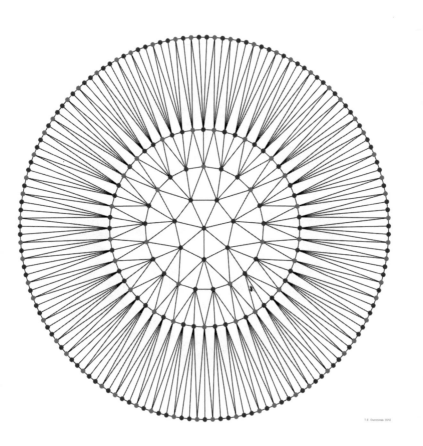

A tessellation of triangles (T. E. Dorczinski, 2010)

An abyss of dodecagons (Baelde, 2012)

Mandelbulb fractal of the North Pole (Ondrej Karlik 2011)

THE FRASER SPIRAL

This was first described by the British psychologist James Fraser in 1908.

Although this appears to be a spiral of twisted cord, you are looking at unconnected concentric circles. Trace them with your finger.

A Fraser spiral illusion (Mysid, 2007)

The sides of this square are straight.

The Ehrenstein illusion

Gestalt illusions

STEREOSCOPE

To see this satellite view in 3D, relax and cross
your eyes slightly so that a third white dot
appears between the two white dots. Shift your
gaze to the photograph beneath the dot. With
practice, a new 3D picture will appear.

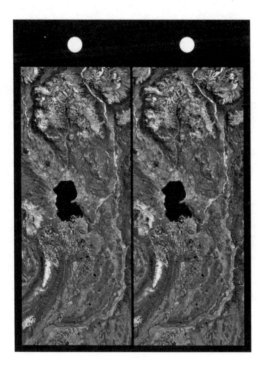

Satellite image of Lake Palanskoye, Kamchatka (NASA, 2012)

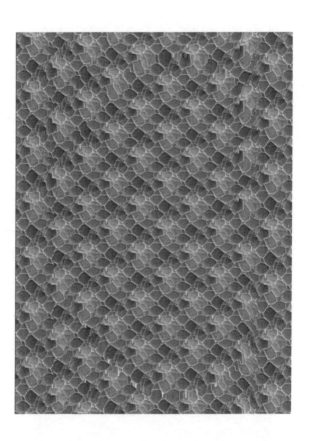

Autostereogram (Martin Havlicek, 2003)

Turn the book so that you are looking at the autostereogram in landscape view.

Relax your eyes again as you did for the last autostereogram.

This time there are no white dots to guide you.
When you unlock the third dimension you will know the answer to this riddle.

A riddle of riddles, it dances and skips,
It is read in the eyes, though it cheats on the lips;
    If it meet with its match it is easily caught;
But when money will buy it, it's not worth a groat.

In 1838, Gustav Fechner described an optical illusion which remains exciting and mysterious.

He designed a number of black and white spinning tops which, when spun, produce unexpected patterns with illusions of depth, light, and colour.

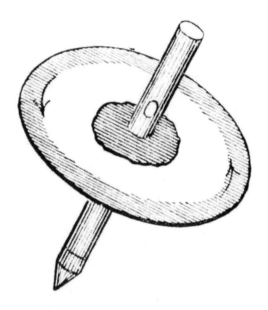

(*Popular Science Monthly*, 1890–1891)

Gustav Fechner (1801–1887)

Author of *The Little Book of Life after Death* (1836)

German physician, physicist, psychologist, chemist, philosopher, riddler, and humorist.

Interests: the senses, pleasure, colour, vision, and enigmas.

MAKE YOUR OWN

Copy the disc onto strong white card.

Cut out.

Use a sharp pencil to pierce the centre of the disc, making a spinning top as in the picture on page 128.

Spin the top and watch colours appear.

The phenomenon is still not fully understood.

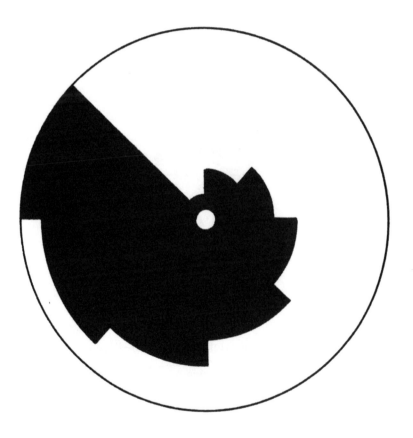

The Fechner disc

In 1866 Helmholtz's *Handbook of Physiological Optics* was published. He describes experiments with spinning tops which generate strange optical effects.

> ... if a disk, marked with black and white sections, be rotated with a certain rapidity, the field appears to be covered with a pattern composed of hexagonal spots; at the part of the field of vision corresponding to the yellow spot, a transverse oval figure is seen. In the centre of this figure is a dark spot surrounded by a black circle. Each of the hexagonal spots is dark with a lighter spot in the centre, and surrounded by a red thread, which appears to be moving in minute drops. The field seems to be pervaded by a greenish hue, which flows toward the yellow spot.

F. W. Edridge-Green, letter to *Nature* (January 1895)

(*Popular Science Monthly*, 1907)

Hermann von Helmholtz (1821–1894)

German physicist, physiologist, and psychologist.

Studying the eye, he invented the opthalmoscope, a device for seeing inside the eye itself.

Interests: sound, vision, colour, energy, and space.

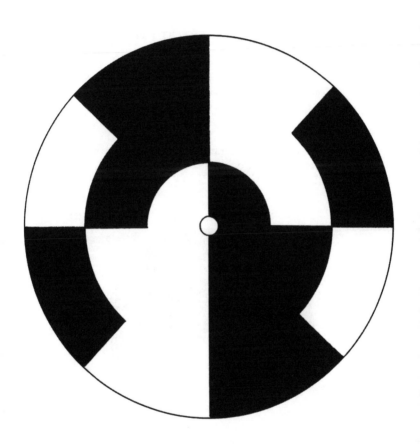

The Helmholtz disc

APPEARING COLOURS

The curious point is that when this disk is revolved, the impression of concentric circles of different colours is produced. If the direction of rotation is reversed, the order of these tints is also reversed.

The cause of these appearances does not appear to have been exactly worked out.

Nature (November 1894)

Benham's artificial spectrum top

(Alma Mater Colcestriensis, 1916)

Charles Benham (1860-1929)

Inventor, journalist, scientist, and inventor of the artificial spectrum top.

When spun, it produces bands of colour in the order of the spectrum.

Interests: the magnet, luminescence, and growing ferns in bottles.

WHAT AM I?

Upon a disk my course I trace,
There restlessly forever flit;
Small is the circuit I embrace,
Two hands suffice to cover it.
Yet ere that field I traverse, I
Full many a thousand mile must go,
E'en though with tempest-speed I fly,
Swifter than arrow from a bow.

Riddle by Johann Schiller (1759-1805)

Answer via code wheel: M GIB27YO

To choose time is to save time.

'Of Dispatch' (1625), Francis Bacon (1561–1626)

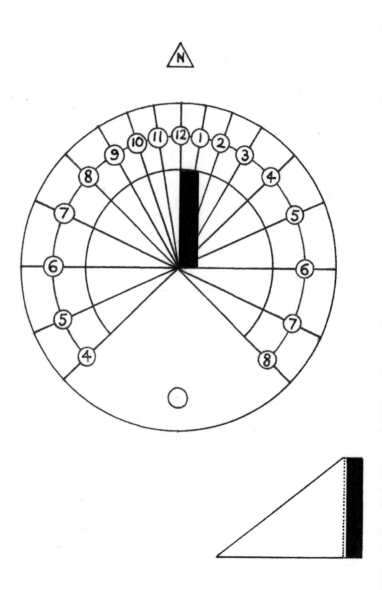

Adapted from work by Donald McGill c.1906

MAKE YOUR OWN SUNDIAL

Make a copy of the dial and the triangular piece to the left (the stile or gnomon) onto stiff card.

Cut out the stile, bend at the dotted line, and glue the black line onto the black line on the dial, with the upright portion aligned to 12 o'clock and standing at an exact right angle.

On a bright day, place the dial flat, with 12 o'clock pointing north.

All colours will agree in the dark.

'Of Unity in Religion' (1625), Francis Bacon (1561–1626)

Better to light a candle than to curse the darkness.

Confucius (c 550- c 478 BC)

THE STRANGE SHADOWS ON THE WALL

It is always interesting to make shadows on the wall, and the pictures on this page show how a great variety of shadows representing animals and people can be made by putting our hands and fingers in certain positions. It takes a little skill to make really good shadows in this way, but all who have patience to practise will be able to make shadows as distinct and clear as those shown here

The World of Wonder (1933)

Illustration by J. J. Grandville (1803–1847) for The Fables of Florian (1842)

143

Why do mirrors
reverse left and right
but not up and down?

HEIDI HOOKE

KICKED

BODIE HICKOX

To find out what happened next, turn this page
upside down and look at it in a mirror.

Ghost-faced bat from *Kunstformen der Natur* (1904) by Ernst Haeckel (1834–1919)

HERMES

MERCURIAL
WONDERS

Mercury (date unknown) by Wenceslaus Hollar (1607–1677)

THE GOD HERMES

The Greek god HERMES (known to the Romans as Mercury) is the god of communication, trade, and trickery.

His interests include: travel, jokes, surprises, codes, crossroads, words, numbers, and ingenuity.

His family includes his alleged son, the god Pan, whose hobby of creeping up on people and scaring them is preserved in the word 'panic'.

Hermes, though a master of disguise, can often be identified by his winged footwear and headwear, and the caduceus: a magic wand around which two snakes curl.

Greek postage stamp (1861)

149

What is black and enlightens the world?

S	A	T	O	R
A	R	E	P	O
T	E	N	E	T
O	P	E	R	A
R	O	T	A	S

The Latin words in this square can be read left and right and up and down. It was discovered carved in stone in Pompei.

ABRACADABRA
ABRACADABR
ABRACADAB
ABRACADA
ABRACAD
ABRACA
ABRAC
ABRA
ABR
AB
A

ABRACADABRA

A lucky charm, widely distributed across the world.

Reading the letters and moving up, down, left, and right, the word ABRACADABRA can be spelled in a multitude of ways.

CHARMS

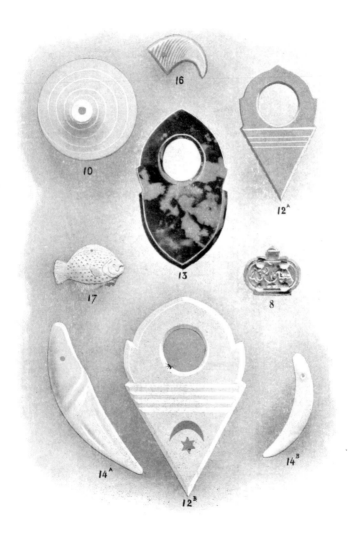

Specimens of trade charms (Folk-Lore: A Quarterly Review of Myth, Tradition, Institution & Customs, 1902)

TWENTY-SIX

Amadou
Fungus used for making fires and healing wounds.

Bathybius
Slime from the bottom of the sea.

Caliology
The study of birds' nests.

Druse
Cavity lined with crystals.

Enchiridion
Handbook.

Frass
Insect faeces.

Galantine
Cold, boned, boiled, spiced white meat.

Hispid
Bristly.

Ichor
Blood of the Olympian gods.

Jocose
Playful.

Kerf
Cut end of tree.

Loricate
Having armour of bone or scales.

Mattamore
Underground house or store.

Novercal
Stepmotherly.

Opsimath
A person who learns late in life.

Persiflage
The art of making important things trivial and trivial things important.

Quaquaversal
Pointing in every direction.

Roofer
Thank you letter.

Serinette
Instrument used to teach caged birds to sing.

Tulcan
A fake cow used to make cows produce milk.

Urticate
Sting with nettles.

Vermian
Worm-like.

Weasand
Windpipe.

Xyster
Instrument for scraping bones.

Yaffle
Green woodpecker.

Zygal
Shaped like the letter 'H'.

The message below is true

The message above is false

A

12 13 14

C

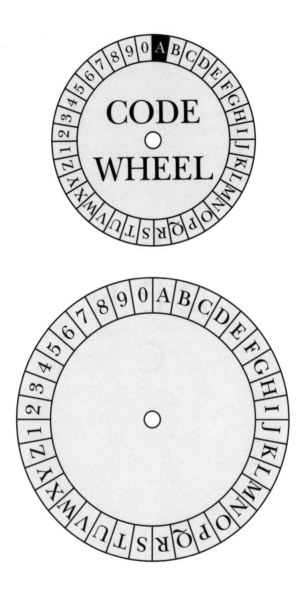

CODE WHEEL

By making a code wheel you will be able to find the answers to some of the riddles in this book. If you make two sets of code wheels you will be able to exchange coded messages with a friend.

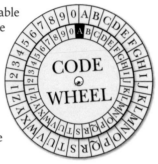

Make a code wheel by copying the two letter-wheels onto cardboard. Fix the two wheels together in the centre using a brad, pin, or tack.

TO ENCODE A MESSAGE

First write down your message, e.g. 'The time is now'.

To encode your message, align the letter 'A' on the inner wheel with any letter or number on the outer wheel, e.g. 'Z'. Keep the letter wheels in place and transcribe your coded message by finding the letters of your original message on the outer wheel and writing down the new letters on the inner wheel. So, with the inner 'A' aligned with the outer 'Z', the letter 'T' is now '5', 'H' is 'S', and 'E' is 'P'. The sentence 'The time is now' will be encoded as '5SP 5TXP T4 YZ8'. For someone to decode your sentence, they will need to know the key. In this case, it is the letter 'Z'. Make sure you write this at the beginning of the message. Thus by aligning the A and the Z on their code wheel, your ally will be able to decode your message by looking for the letters on the inner wheel and writing down the corresponding letters on the outer wheel.

Try this one out, remembering that the first letter or number is the key telling you where to align the inner A:

5 OL GZ LOXYZ 5U1 JUTZ Y1IIKKJ ZX5 ZX5 ZX5 GMGOT

INVISIBLE INK

In his book *Mercury, or the Secret and Swift Messenger* (1641), a study of codes and long-distance communication, John Wilkins (1614–1672) provides a recipe for invisible ink that uses crushed glow worms.

Glow worms are too precious to sacrifice for human communications. Far more effective for secret communication are these substances:

1. The juice of a lemon. Use fresh juice to write on paper using a toothpick or dip pen and let it dry. To read the message, place the paper in direct sunlight or warm carefully over a radiator.

2. A solution of bicarbonate of soda. Mix one teaspoon of bicarbonate of soda with one tablespoon of water. Use a toothpick or dip pen to write your message on white paper and let it dry. The message can be read by mixing two drops of food colouring with a teaspoon of water and painting this over the paper with a paintbrush.

Female glowworm (*Nordisk familjebok*, 1912)

Rongorongo script transcribed by Thomas Barthel (1923-1997)

This is *Rongorongo*, the written language found on Easter Island.

The meaning remains mysterious, and all we have are guesses.

The symbols are thought to be *logograms*, where each symbol is a picture of an object or artefact.

From *Easter Island and Its Mysteries* (1935) by Dr Stéphen Chauvet

Secrecy (date unknown) by Wenceslas Hollar (1607-1677)

Hermes, as the god of secrecy and communications, presides over messages sent between lovers. The message below was sent on a postcard in 1936.

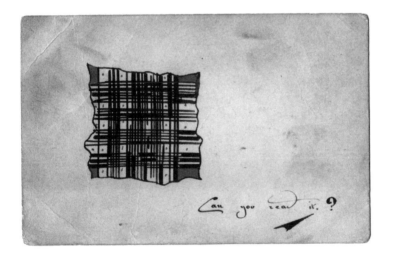

Hand-drawn postcard from the author's collection

A short saying often contains much wisdom.

Sophocles (496–406 BC), *Aletes*, Fragment 99 (date unknown)

All good things must come to an end.

Beauty is in the eye of the beholder.

Believe nothing of what you hear,
and only half of what you see.

Books and friends should be few but good.

A chain is no stronger than its weakest link.

Don't count your chickens before they're hatched.

Don't put all your eggs in one basket.

Even a worm can turn.

Every cloud has a silver lining.

Every picture tells a story.

Experience is the best teacher.

The eye is bigger than the belly.

Forgive and forget.

Great oaks from little acorns grow.

A hedge between keeps friendship green.

It is easy to be wise after the event.

It will all be the same in a hundred years.

Keep something for a rainy day.

Knowledge is power.

Laughter is the best medicine.

Live and learn.

Love laughs at locksmiths.

Make hay while the sun shines.

Many a true word is spoken in jest.

Necessity is the mother of invention.

Never judge from appearances.

Never too late to learn.

Seeing is believing.

Things are not always what they seem.

Time will tell.

You can't please everyone.

Illustration by George Roux (c.1850–1929) for the novel *The Sphinx of the Ice Fields* (1897) by Jules Verne (1828–1905)

WHAT ARE WE?

We are little airy Creatures,
All of diff'rent Voice and Features.
One of us in Glass is set,
One of us you'll find in Jet,
T'other you may see in Tin,
And the fourth a Box within.
If the fifth you should pursue
It can never fly from You.

Jonathan Swift (1667–1745)

Answer via code wheel: E RKSAHO

You went into the woods and got one.

You sat down to find it.

When you could not find it,
you took it home with you.

What was it?

Answer via code wheel: Q C0G38DYB

HOMER KILLED BY THIS RIDDLE?

What we caught we threw away;
what we didn't catch we kept.

This riddle was posed to the poet Homer (dates of birth and death unknown, *c.*8th century BC) by fishermen on the Greek island of Ios.

It is said that stress brought on by this riddle caused Homer's death. You, however, need only turn a wheel for the comfort of an answer.

Answer via code wheel: Z QWPL4 Z3 WTVP

Alive without breath,
As cold as death;
Never thirsty, ever drinking,
All in mail never clinking.

Riddle from *The Hobbit* (1937), John Ronald Reuel Tolkien (1892–1973)

Answer via code wheel: H 9BLA

1. What gets bigger the more you take away from it?

2. What gets longer when it is cut at both ends?

3. Why is a loaf of bread on top of a mountain like a very valuable horse?

4. Why is the tip of a dog's tail like the heart of a tree?

5. Why is a room full of married people like an empty one?

6. Why is a freshly baked loaf like a caterpillar?

7. What is the difference between a jailer and a jeweller?

8. Why is a mouse like hay?

9. What is stationary when it is alive and walks about when it is dead?

10. What question must you always answer 'no' to?

You may find me there before you at anybody's door,
In the palace of the rich or the cottage of the poor;
You may find me in the earth and air, but in the mighty sea
Would surely be a place, my friends,
you need not look for me.
I've lived out in the country, and I've lived within the town.
And moved so oft from house to house I long to settle down.
Both men and women shun me, the youthful and the old
(But oh! how glad to grasp me when I am made of gold).
I hate the winter's ice and snow and hate to have it rain
I'm very fond of travelling and I'm always on a train.

The Fireside Book of Riddles (early 20th century)

Answer via code wheel: V S089

Londoners and visitors to London see this word a lot.

The word has eleven letters.

Its first three letters are the same as its last three letters, although they are not in the same order.

The middle five letters of the word are ERGRO.

What is the word?

Answer via code wheel Z GYOP3R3ZGYO

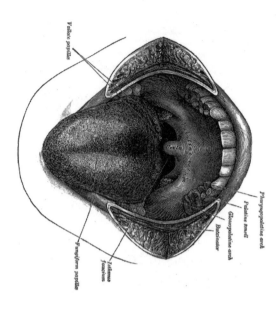

From *Gray's Anatomy of the Human Body* (1918) by Henry Gray (1827-1861)

Vallate papilla

Pharyngopalatine arch

Palatine tonsil

Glossopalatine arch

Buccinator

Isthmus faucium

Fungiform papillae

Walter Waddle won a Walking Wager.
Did Walter Waddle win a Walking Wager?
If Walter Waddle won a Walking Wager,
Where's the Walking Wager Walter Waddle won?

Peter Piper's Practical Principles of Plain and Perfect Pronunciation. (1836)

Kuku

kaki

kiriku

kaku–

ku

kikis

kuku

kaki

kiriku.

Translation: My left toenail is stiff – I scrape my left toenail.

Malaysian tongue twister

TONGUE TWISTERS

IN OTHER TONGUES

Kupa me kapak kupa pa kapak.
The cup with a lid, the cup without a lid.

Albanian

Le ver vert va vers le verre vert.
The green worm goes towards the green glass.

French

Pitumput-pitong puting pating.
Seventy-seven white sharks.

Filipino

TO BE READ ALOUD

Red leather, yellow leather
Red leather, yellow leather
Red leather, yellow leather.

A glowing gleam growing green.

Purple, paper, people,
Purple, people, paper,
People, purple, paper,
Paper, purple, people.

Six thick thistle sticks.

PALINDROMES

Read these words and sentences backwards:

EYE

RACECAR

LIVE NOT ON EVIL

WAS IT A CAR OR A CAT I SAW?

SUMS ARE NOT SET AS A TEST ON ERASMUS

AMBIGRAMS

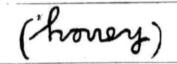

ARE THERE OTHERS?

A S you will notice, the slang word "chump," if written in the manner here shown, reads the same even when held upside down. I think it is the only word in the English language which has this peculiarity, and therefore hope you will consider it worthy of insertion in your "Curiosities" column.— Mr. Mitchell T. Lavin, 931, West Ninth Street, Cincinnati, Ohio, U.S.A.

ANOTHER "REVERSIBLE" WORD.

L AST month you gave an example of a word so written that it read the same when turned

upside down. Such words are very few and far between, but I have succeeded in discovering another, for which I hope you will be able to find a corner.— Mr. V. K. Allison, Lawrenceville School, Lawrenceville, New Jersey, U.S.A.

ANAGRAM

An anagram is a word or phrase with its letters rearranged. It comes from the Greek 'write again' (*ana* again or anew; *grapho* write).

Lemon = melon

Plum = lump

Peach = cheap

Aspire = praise

Cheat = teach

Death = hated

Deaf = fade

Listen = silent

Conversation = voices rant on

Monday = dynamo

Thousand = handouts

Night = thing

Astronomer = moon starer *or* no more stars

Elation = toenail

A SHAMAN AT RISING
by Cam Lam Twelfth

A giant man's hairs.
Martian has a sign.
A hangman is astir.
'*Sin*,' saith a ragman
'has a smart gain in
Harming, as a stain.
Aim, Host a-snaring.
A Satan arming his
Ants, rash again am I.'
A saint has margin.
As a garish tin man
Hangs a simian rat.
A maharani stings.
In a saga isn't harm.
This is an anagram.

Every line of this poem, including the title, is an anagram of the phrase 'this is an anagram'.

179

Rearrange these letters to make one word:

NOW RED

Rearrange these letters to make one word:

NOW REDO

COMMUNICATING
ACROSS DISTANCES

The word **telephone** comes from the Greek for 'far sound'.

(*tele* far, *phone* sound).

Advertisement, 1910

SENDING MESSAGES BY STRING

In *Mercury, or the Secret and Swift Messenger* (1641), John Wilkins (1614–1672) describes a method of writing and reading messages by making marks on string.

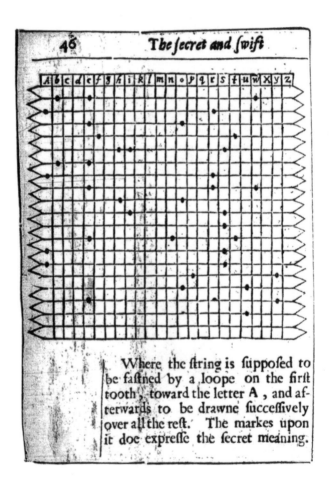

A way of learning Morse code, based on the work of Arnold and Max Reinhold (date unknown)

A •—	U ••—
B —•••	V •••—
C —•—•	W •——
D —••	X —••—
E •	Y —•——
F ••—•	Z ——••
G ——•	
H ••••	
I ••	
J •———	
K —•—	0 —————
L •—••	1 ••————
M ——	2 •••———
N —•	3 •••——
O ———	4 ••••—
P •——•	5 •••••
Q ——•—	6 —••••
R •—•	7 ——•••
S •••	8 ———••
T —	9 —————•

Morse code

INTERNATIONAL MORSE CODE

1. A dash is equal to three dots.

2. The space between parts of the same letter is equal to one dot.

3. The space between two letters is equal to three dots.

4. The space between two words is equal to seven dots.

'The Morse code' is an anagram of 'Here come dots.'

Morse Postcard from the author's collection

Samuel Finley Breese Morse (1791–1872), artist and co-inventor of Morse code.

Portrait of Samuel Morse (1866) by Mathew Brady (c.1822–1896)

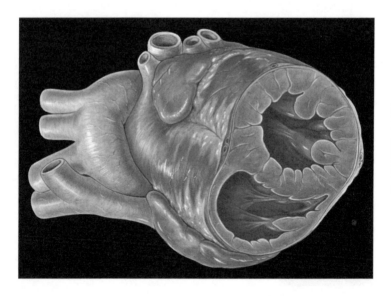

Heart (Patrick J. Lynch, 2006)

Arithmetria (1519) by Hans Sebald Beham (1500–1550)

Multiplication is vexation,
Division is as bad;
The rule of three doth puzzle me,
And practice drives me mad.

Elizabethan rhyme, Anonymous

How long would it take you to count to one million, if you counted at the rate of one per second, and did not take any breaks?

How long would it take you to count to one billion, if you counted at the rate of one per second, and did not take any breaks?

THE CURIOSITY SHOP MYSTERY

Three brothers visited a Curiosity Shop and wished to buy a game.

The friendly shopkeeper told the brothers the game cost £30.

The brothers thought this was a bargain.

They each gave the shopkeeper a £10 note.

As they were leaving the shop, the brothers noticed a price label inside the game: 'GAME: £25'.

The shopkeeper gave the brothers an apology and five £1 coins.

Each of the brothers took a £1 coin, and decided to give the shopkeeper the remaining two £1 coins because he was so friendly.

That means each brother paid £9. Three times nine equals twenty-seven. They gave the shopkeeper £2. Twenty-seven plus two equals twenty-nine.

What happened to the other pound?

1	3	5	7	9	11	13	15
17	19	21	23	25	27	29	31
33	35	37	39	41	43	45	47
49	51	53	55	57	59	61	63

2	3	6	7	10	11	14	15
18	19	22	23	26	27	30	31
34	35	38	39	42	43	46	47
50	51	54	55	58	59	62	63

4	5	6	7	12	13	14	15
20	21	22	23	28	29	30	31
36	37	38	39	44	45	46	47
52	53	54	55	60	61	62	63

8	9	10	11	12	13	14	15
24	25	26	27	28	29	30	31
40	41	42	43	44	45	46	47
56	57	58	59	60	61	62	63

16	17	18	19	20	21	22	23
24	25	26	27	28	29	30	31
48	49	50	51	52	53	54	55
56	57	58	59	60	61	62	63

32	33	34	35	36	37	38	39
40	41	42	43	44	45	46	47
48	49	50	51	52	53	54	55
56	57	58	59	60	61	62	63

SECRET NUMBER CARDS

Make yourself a set of the cards opposite by copying them onto cardboard. Then all you need is a friend and a table.

1. Have a friend choose any card.

2. Have your friend choose any number from this card without revealing the number to you. Place the card face up on the table.

3. Show your friend the other cards, one at a time. If they see their number they are to tell you, but they are not to reveal the number.

4. As you do this, make two face-up piles on the table, one pile with cards that show the chosen number, one pile with cards that do not.

5. To find out the secret number, look through the pile of cards that your friend has told you show their number. If you add together the numbers in the top left-hand corners the total will be the secret number.

6. Tell your friend their secret number. If you have been quick and accurate, they will be impressed. Keep the method secret.

7. With practice and focus, you can add up the cards as you go along. This way you won't need a table. But you will still need a friend.

8. Battle mode: Become a Lighting Calculator. When you meet someone who has a set of these cards or who knows the method, challenge them to an 'add-off'. Test one another's speed and accuracy. Practice makes perfect.

COUNT YOUR BLESSINGS

You will need to be quite rich to try this out.

YOU WILL NEED:

25 copper coins
25 silver coins
A bag or box
A table or floor

INSTRUCTIONS:

1. Sit.
2. Breathe.
3. Mix up the coins in the bag or box.
4. Without looking, reach into the bag or box and remove two coins at random at the same time.
5. Look at the coins. If they are both copper coins, put them in a pile on your left. If they are both silver coins, put them in a pile on your right. If they are one of each, put them in a pile directly in front of you.
6. Repeat Steps 4 and 5 until you have used up all of the coins by making three separate piles.
7. Make a wish.
8. Put the middle pile of mixed coins back in the bag or box without counting them.
9. Count the coins in the left hand pile of copper coins.
10. Count the coins in the right hand pile of silver coins.
11. If the number of copper coins is the same as the number of silver coins, TODAY IS YOUR LUCKY DAY.

Melencolia I (1514) by Albrecht Dürer (1471–1528)

DÜRER'S MELANCHOLY

Below can be seen a MAGIC SQUARE.

The bottom middle two numbers show the year in which Dürer made this engraving: 1514.

The square has remarkable properties.

Every row of numbers adds up to 34.

Every column of numbers adds up to 34.

The diagonals add up to 34.

The four corner numbers add up to 34.

The four centre numbers add up to 34.

There are even more ways.

The picture on the next page shows how.

16	3	2	13
5	10	11	8
9	6	7	12
4	15	14	1

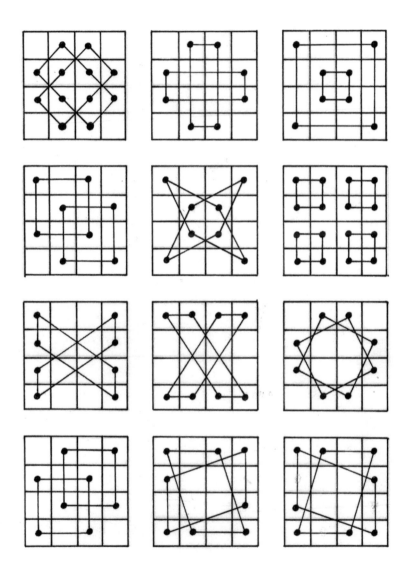

The many ways the number 34 can be totalled on Dürer's magic square

DAEDALUS

WONDERFUL
CONSTRUCTIONS

The Golden Mean (date unknown) by Wenceslas Hollar (1607–1677)

DAEDALUS, a semi-mythical Athenian who spent much of his life living on different islands, was a remarkable inventor.

Inventions associated with Daedalus include:

The maze

The labyrinth

The clew, a ball of string which assists in the navigation of mazes

The saw and the comb (possibly invented by his nephew after he found a fish bone on the beach)

The spinning top

Compasses

An umbrella activated by rain or intense sunshine

The marionette

Puzzles

Knots

Wings for humans

Automata, including the giant metal guardian Talos who was powered by ichor

A CHAOS EXPERIMENT

Try this out – it might surprise you.

Make up a set of the cards from the facing page. Enlarge and print the page onto cardboard. Cut out the cards. Glue them onto index cards or playing cards. Follow these instructions.

1. Look through the cards in your hand.

2. Smile.

3. Arrange the cards so that BUTTERFLIES alternate with PATTERNS.

4. Hold the cards together as a small pack, and keep them face up.

5. *Without looking at the cards* follow these instructions (you can hold them under the table, or hold them behind your back, or close your eyes and have someone read out the instructions for you).

6. Cut the cards three times.

7. Take off the top card, turn it over, and place it back on top.

8. Take the top two cards together, turn them over, and place them back on top.

9. Take the top three cards together, turn them over, and place them back on top.

10. Take the top four cards together, turn them over, and place them back on top.

11. Take the top five cards together (all but the bottom card), turn them over, and place them back on top.

12. Turn the whole pack over once or twice.

13. Take the top three cards, turn them over, and place them back on top.

14. Take the top card and put it under the second card.

15. Turn the pack over once.

16. Take the top card and put it under the second card.

17. Move three cards from the top to the bottom. Move them either one at a time, or as a group.

18. Turn the whole packet over.

19. From disorder comes order.

20. Tap the cards twice.

21. Look at the cards.

22. Smile.

THE PHAISTOS DISC

Discovered on Crete and of uncertain age, this disc (a replica of which is shown here, both sides) has not yet been deciphered.

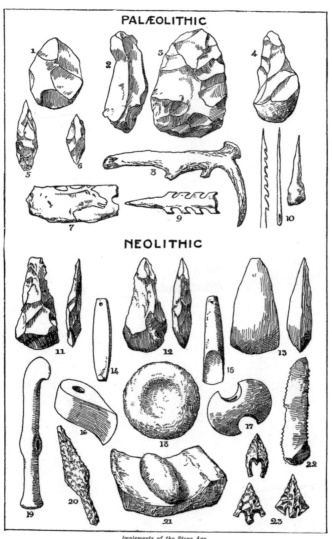

PALÆOLITHIC

NEOLITHIC

Implements of the Stone Age.

Palæolithic:—1. Earliest form of flint implement. 2-4. Typical Palæolithic flint implements. 5. Flint spear-head. 6. Flint arrow-head. 7. Bone engraved with figure of deer. 8-10. Implements of horn and bone. **Neolithic:—**11. Implement chipped only. 12. Implement with working edge ground. 13. Implement ground and polished. 14. Hone. 15. Gouge. 16, 17. Polished axe-heads. 18. Hand-hammer. 19. Axe-hammer. 20. Spear-head. 21. Saddle quern. 22. Saw. 23. Arrow-head. (Drawn from examples in British Museum.)

Stone tools (*The Harmsworth Encyclopedia: Everybody's Book of Reference. c.1905*)

To invent, you need a good imagination and a pile of junk.

Attributed to Thomas Edison (1847–1931)

Nothing great was ever achieved without enthusiasm.

'Circles' (1841) Ralph Waldo Emerson (1803–1882)

FLYING PIGEON SPINNING TOP

MAKE YOUR OWN

1. Copy the disc onto strong white card.

2. Cut out.

3. Use a sharp pencil to pierce the centre of the disc, making a spinning top as in the picture.

4. Spin the top and watch the pigeons fly.

from Descriptive Zoopraxography or the Science of Animal Locomotion Made Popular (1893) by Eadweard Muybridge (1830–1904)

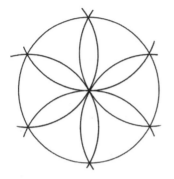

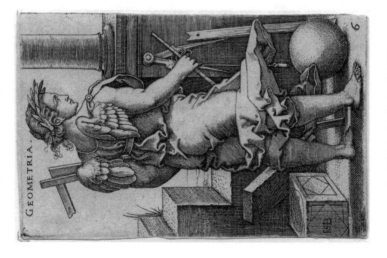

Geometria. (1529) by Hans Sebald Beham. (1500–1550)

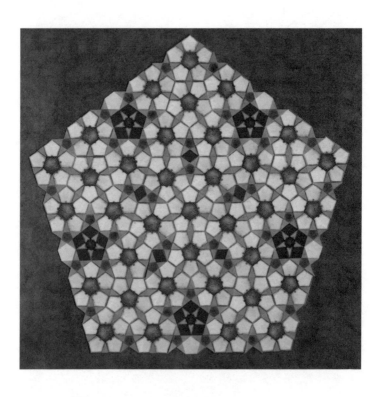

Spring Flowers (2005) by Matthew McFall

Simple Construction of intricate Arab lattice & tile Patterns

The Anatomy of Pattern (1887) by Lewis Foreman Day (1845-1910)

Straight lines

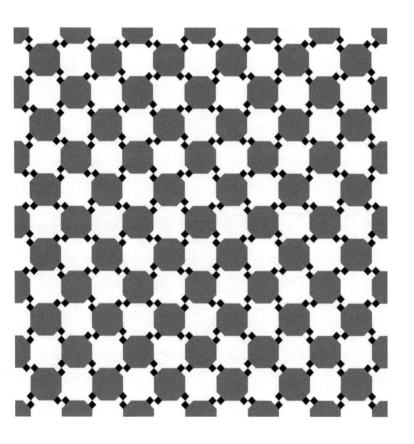

Perpendicular grid

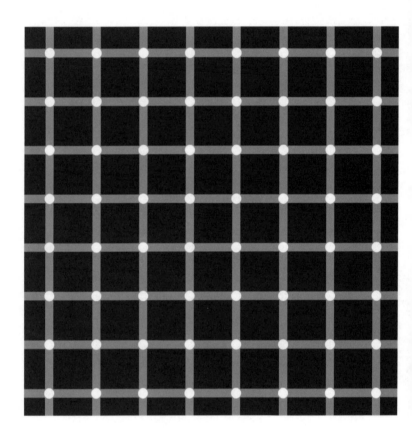

Flashing intersections

What is the difference between a maze and a labyrinth?

A MAZE is a trap for the unwary which offers many choices of path. It is possible to get very lost in a maze.

A LABYRINTH has only one path from the entrance to the centre. It is impossible to get lost, although the experience of walking a labyrinth can be puzzling and disorienting. This is in part due to the many compact twists and turns of the path which affect your inner ear (itself partly a labyrinth) and your sense of proprioception.

Labyrinths are 'grown' from a seed pattern of five points arranged in a pattern called the quincunx.

This book will show you how to construct a labyrinth.

Labyrinths are worth making ...

Last night I dreamt I was in the labyrinth,
And woke far on. I did not know the place.

'The Labyrinth' (1949), Edwin Muir (1887–1959)

Labyrinth (date unknown) by Wolf Helmhardt von Hohberg (1612–1688)

COMMENCE WITH
A QUINCUNX

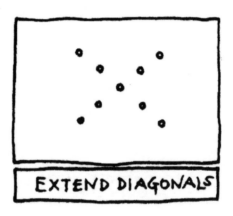

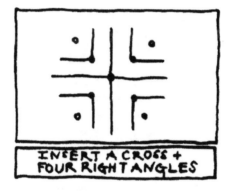

INSERT A CROSS +
FOUR RIGHT ANGLES

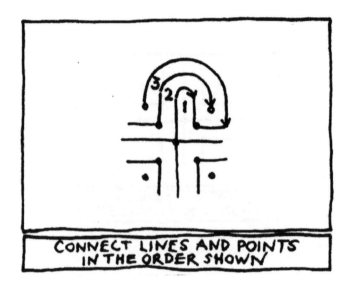

CONNECT LINES AND POINTS
IN THE ORDER SHOWN

CONTINUE TO MAKE CONNECTIONS

THE LABYRINTH COMPLETE

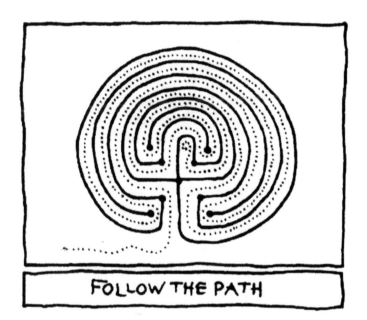

FOLLOW THE PATH

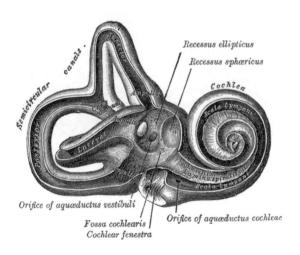

The osseus labyrinth your inner ear from Gray's Anatomy of the Human Body (1918) by Henry Gray (1827–1861)

Vein skeleton of hydrangea (LuuLy, 2008)

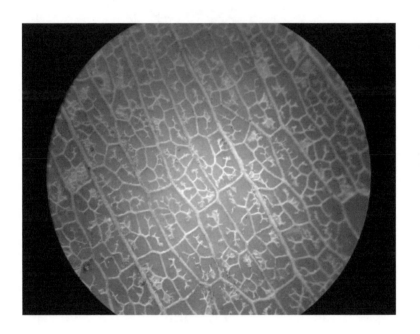

Leaf skeleton (Julian Herzog, 2006)

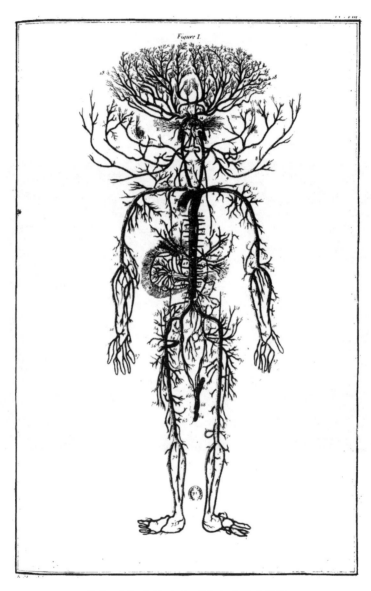

Blood vessels from the *Encyclopedia of Diderot and d'Alembert* (1762)

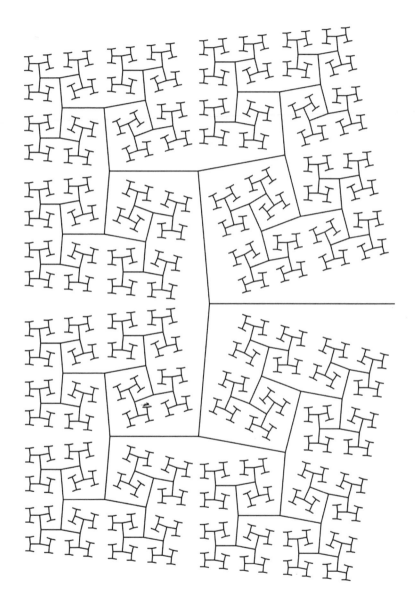

(Murry Puzzle, 2008)

GET LOST AND FIND YOURSELF

A complex maze to explore by eye or with pencil.

Scan, enlarge, and print a copy of the maze.

Mark a cross anywhere.

Choose a place in the maze far away from the cross you made.

Now follow the paths and find the cross.

You can use a pencil or follow the paths with your eyes.

If you come out at the sides, return by any door.

The reward of patience is patience.

St Augustine (354–430)

THE BOOMERANG ILLUSION

Scan and print these two boomerangs onto heavy cardboard and cut them out.

Decorate them so that each is different.

You will notice that if you place them next to one another, the boomerang placed on the left will look bigger than the boomerang on the right.

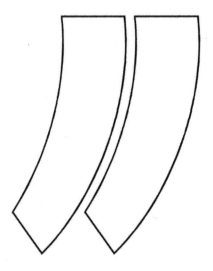

A PUZZLE FOR YOU TO MAKE

Scan and print or copy this triangle puzzle onto heavy cardboard.

Cut out the four pieces of the triangle with precision.

Rearrange the pieces as shown in B.

Can you account for the missing square?

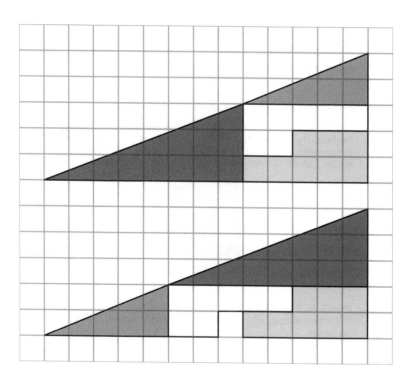

No. XIII.—The Greek Cross Puzzle.

Given, a piece of paper or cardboard in the form of a Greek or equal-armed cross, as Fig. 175.

Fig. 175.

Required, by two straight cuts so to divide it that the pieces when reunited shall form a square.

No. XIV.—The Protean Puzzle.

This is a puzzle of the same class as the Anchor, Tormentor, and Pythagoras (pp. 77–83), but very much easier, from the greater number of the component parts. It consists of eleven pieces of cardboard, forming an oblong square, as

Fig. 176.

shown in Fig. 176. Figs. 177–182 illustrate a few only of the many shapes which can be constructed out of the above elements.

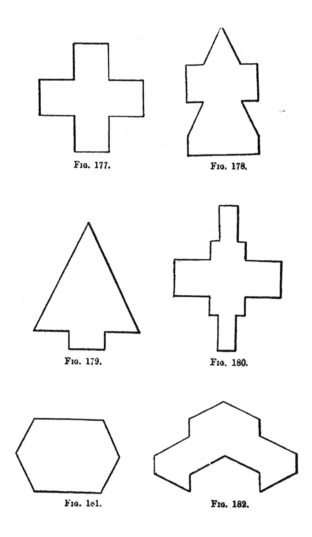

FIG. 177.

FIG. 178.

FIG. 179.

FIG. 180.

FIG. 181.

FIG. 182.

From *Puzzles Old and New* (1893) by Professor Hoffmann (1839–1919)

THINKING OUTSIDE THE BOX

This puzzle, shown here on a postcard, is the origin of the phrase 'Thinking outside the box'.

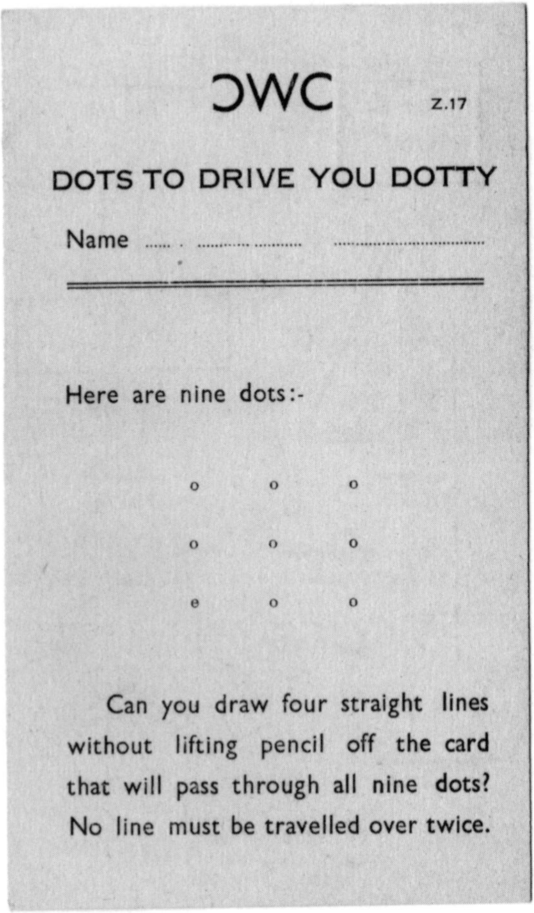

ƆWC   Z.17

DOTS TO DRIVE YOU DOTTY

Name ....

Here are nine dots:-

   o   o   o

   o   o   o

   e   o   o

Can you draw four straight lines without lifting pencil off the card that will pass through all nine dots? No line must be travelled over twice.

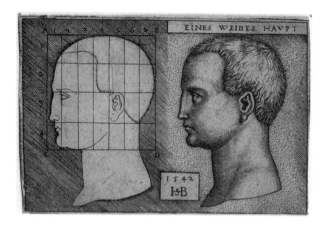

Eines Weibes Haupt by Hans Sebald Beham (1500–1550)

Landscape by Wenceslas Hollar (1607–1677)

VALEDICTION

En cap cap cap el que cap en aquest cap.

Catalan tongue twister:
In no head enters what enters in this head.

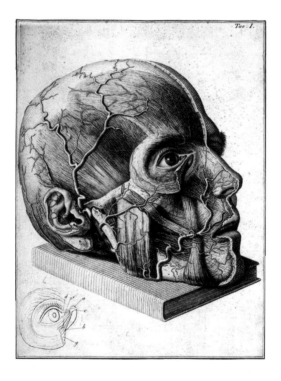

from A Treatise on the Principle Diseases of the Eye (1801) by Antonio Scarpa (1752–1832)

Return and look again ... take a fresh, attentive look at the greatness, beauty, harmony, strength, and variety of the whole great fabric of Creation. Usually we feel no admiration because there is no novelty, and without admiration there is no attentiveness. We all enter the World with the eyes of the mind closed, and by the time we open them to knowledge, the custom of things, no matter how marvellous they are, leaves no room for Wonder. The wise have always drawn on reflection, imagining themselves newly arrived in the World, pausing over its prodigies—for each thing is one — admiring perfection and ingeniously philosophizing. Just as someone strolling through the most delightful of gardens goes distractedly down its paths without noticing the loveliness of its plants or the variety of its flowers, and then, noticing, turns around and begins to delight, one by one, in each and every plant and flower, so it is with us: we travel from the cradle to the grave scarcely noticing the beauty and perfection of this Universe. The wise always turn round, renewing their enjoyment and contemplating each thing with fresh attention, if not new sight.

Baltasar Gracián (1601–1658), *The Hero* (1637)

Everything has its wonders, even darkness and silence, and I learn, whatever state I may be in, therein to be content.

Helen Keller (1880–1968), deaf and blind from infancy

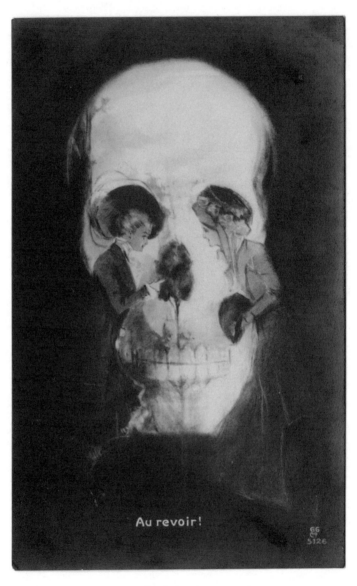

Au revoir! postcard (no date) from the author's collection

IMAGE CREDITS

Title page, 7, 15, 45, 105, 145, 195: *Fertilising Cornucopia* (1895) by R. Christiansen. Available under Creative Commons Attribution/Share-A-Like Licence

Page i: © Ian Gilbert

Page iv: Albrecht Altdorfer (*c.*1480–1538). Available under Creative Commons Attribution/Share-A-Like Licence

Page 1: Anatomy of the head, lateral view. By permission of Patrick J. Lynch, 2006. Available under Creative Commons Attribution/Share-A-Like Licence

Page 2: *Trompe l'oeil* by Cornelis Norbertus Gijsbrechts (fl. 1660–1683). Courtesy of the Museum of Fine Arts, Ghent. Available under Creative Commons Attribution/Share-A-Like Licence

Page 3: *The Widow* (date unknown) by Frederick Dielman (1847–1935). Courtesy of the Boston Public Library/Louis Prang & Co. Collection

Page 4: Yellowknife Bay, the landing site of NASA's *Curiosity* rover. By permission of NASA, 2012. Available under Creative Commons Attribution/Share-A-Like Licence

Page 6: Illustration by Sir John Tenniel (1820–1914) for the first edition of *Alice in Wonderland* (1865). Available under Creative Commons Attribution/Share-A-Like Licence

Page 10: Illustration from *Wondertooneel der Natuur*, Vol. 2 (Levinus Vincent, 1715). Available under Creative Commons Attribution/Share-A-Like Licence

Page 11: Ferrante Imperato (*c.*1525–*c.*1615), *Dell'Historia Naturale* (1599). Available under Creative Commons Attribution/Share-A-Like Licence

Page 12: Ole Worm's Cabinet of Curiosities, *Museum Wormianum* (1655). Courtesy of the Smithsonian Institute Libraries, Washington, D.C.

Page 13: Illustration from *Wondertooneel der Natuur*, Vol. 1 (Levinus Vincent, 1715). Available under Creative Commons Attribution/Share-A-Like Licence

Page 14: *Cabinet of Curiosities* (1690) by Domenico Remps. Courtesy of the Museo dell'Opificio delle Pietre Dure, Florence

Page 16, 17: *Aristaeus and Proteus* (date unknown) by Wenceslas Hollar (1607–1677). Available under Creative Commons Attribution/Share-A-Like Licence

Page 18: Scanning electron micrograph. Source Eugene Karl Kempf, 2012. Available under Creative Commons Attribution Licence

Page 19: *Sphinx Mystagoga* (1676) by Athanasius Kircher (*c.*1602–1680). Available under Creative Commons Attribution/Share-A-Like Licence

Page 20: Fractal growth. Source Solkoll, 2005. Available under Creative Commons Attribution/Share-A-Like Licence

Page 21: Koch flake. Available under Creative Commons Attribution/Share-A-Like Licence

Page 22: Koch snowflake. Available under Creative Commons Attribution/Share-A-Like Licence

Page 23: *Heraclitus and Democritus* (1477) by Donato Bramante (1444–1514). Under licence from Italian Ministry for Cultural Goods and Activities

Page 24: List of elements (1808) by John Dalton (1766–1844). Available under Creative Commons Attribution/Share-A-Like Licence

Page 25: Babbitt's model of the atom from *Principles of Light and Colour* (1878) by Edwin D. Babbitt (1828–1905). Available under Creative Commons Attribution/Share-A-Like Licence

Page 26: Model of the atom by Ernest Rutherford (1871–1937). Available under Creative Commons Attribution/Share-A-Like Licence

Page 26: Model of the atom (*The World of Wonder*, 1932)

Page 30: A field ion microscope image of platinum atoms. Source Tasuo Iwata, 2006. Available under Creative Commons Attribution/Share-A-Like Licence

Page 31: Auntie Mary scrubbing the floor. By permission of John Farnsbarns, 2012

Page 31: Structure of a water molecule (H_2O). Source Solkoll, 2005. Available under Creative Commons Attribution/Share-A-Like Licence

Page 32: *Micrographia* (1665) by Robert Hooke (1635–1703). Available under Creative Commons Attribution/Share-A-Like Licence

Page 33: Protein crystals grown in space. By permission of NASA, 2000. Available under Creative Commons Attribution/Share-A-Like Licence

Page 34: One of the first ever X-ray radiograms (Wilhelm Röntgen, 1845–1923). Available under Creative Commons Attribution/Share-A-Like Licence

Page 35: James Clerk Maxwell (1831–1879) holding the colour-matching disc he invented. Available under Creative Commons Attribution/Share-A-Like Licence

Page 35: Spherical harmonic of the third degree, James Clerk Maxwell (*A Treatise on Electricity and Magnetism*, 1873). Available under Creative Commons Attribution/Share-A-Like Licence

Page 36: Lissajous figure – a mathematical curve. Source Solkoll, 2005. Available under Creative Commons Attribution/Share-A-Like Licence

Page 37: How sounds are made visible to the eye (*The World of Wonder*, 1933)

Pages 38–40: How to make a Wondergraph (H. H. Windsor, *The Boy Mechanic*, 1913)

Page 41: Jules Lissajous (1822–1880). Available under Creative Commons Attribution/Share-A-Like Licence

Page 42: Stardust fragment caught in aerogel. By permission of NASA, 2006. Available under Creative Commons Attribution/Share-A-Like Licence

Page 43: Corpuscles of dust (*Popular Science Monthly*, 1876)

Page 46: 'What an Aquarium Should Be' (*Illustrated Sporting and Dramatic News*, 1876). Available under Creative Commons Attribution/Share-A-Like Licence

Page 48: *Selection of Shells Arranged on Shelves* (*Choix de coquillages*) (early 19th century) by Alexandre Isidore Leroy de Barde (1777–1828). (C) RMN-Grand Palais (musée du Louvre)

Page 49: *Water* (1566) by Giuseppe Arcimboldo (1527–1593). Courtesy of the Kunsthistorisches Museum, Vienna (Wien)

Page 50: *Bathykorus bouilloni*. By permission of the US Oceanic and Atmospheric Administration, 2005. Available under Creative Commons Attribution/Share-A-Like Licence

Page 51: Photograph of giant squid in bath tub, Logy Bay, Newfoundland (1873). Available under Creative Commons Attribution/Share-A-Like Licence

Page 52: Mrs Gren? (no date), author's collection

Page 55: Types of diatoms (*The Harmsworth Encyclopedia: Everybody's Book of Reference*, c.1905)

Page 56: *Diatomea* from *Kunstformen der Natur* (1904) by Ernst Haeckel (1834–1919). Available under Creative Commons Attribution/Share-A-Like Licence

Page 59: *Anatomy of a Pregnant Woman* (1773) by Jacques Fabien Gautier D'Agoty (1716–1785) Courtesy of the National Library of Medicine, Bethesda, Maryland. Available under Creative Commons Attribution/Share-A-Like Licence

Page 61: Oeufs from *Nouveau Larousse Illustré*, Vol. 6 (1897–1904) by Adolphe Millot (1857–1921). Available under Creative Commons Attribution/Share-A-Like Licence

Page 62: Anatomy of an egg. By permission of Horst Frank, 2008. Available under Creative Commons Attribution/Share-A-Like Licence

Page 63: The larva of the ox head flatworm from *Kunstformen der Natur* (1904) by Ernst Haeckel (1834–1919). Available under Creative Commons Attribution/Share-A-Like Licence

Page 64: Pythagoras tree. By permission of Guillaume Jacquernot, 2010. Available under Creative Commons Attribution/Share-A-Like Licence

Page 65: Lichens from *Kunstformen der Natur* (1904) by Ernst Haeckel (1834–1919). Available under Creative Commons Attribution/Share-A-Like Licence

Page 66: *Glaucus lineatus* (1868) by Rudolph Bergh (1824–1909). Available under Creative Commons Attribution/Share-A-Like Licence

Page 67: *Bryozoa* from *Kunstformen der Natur* (1904) by Ernst Haeckel (1834–1919). Available under Creative Commons Attribution/Share-A-Like Licence

Page 67: *Phaeodaria* from *Kunstformen der Natur* (1904) by Ernst Haeckel (1834–1919). Available under Creative Commons Attribution/Share-A-Like Licence

Page 68: *Amphoridea* from *Kunstformen der Natur* (1904) by Ernst Haeckel (1834–1919). Available under Creative Commons Attribution/Share-A-Like Licence

Page 68: *Ophiodea* from *Kunstformen der Natur* (1904) by Ernst Haeckel (1834–1919). Available under Creative Commons Attribution/Share-A-Like Licence

Page 69: *Spirobranchia* from *Kunstformen der Natur* (1904) by Ernst Haeckel (1834–1919). Available under Creative Commons Attribution/Share-A-Like Licence

Page 69: *Cirripedia* from *Kunstformen der Natur* (1904) by Ernst Haeckel (1834–1919). Available under Creative Commons Attribution/Share-A-Like Licence

Page 70: *The Crab and its Mother* (1668) by Wenceslas Hollar (1607–1677). Available under Creative Commons Attribution/Share-A-Like Licence

Page 71: Japanese spider crab (*Popular Science Magazine*, 1920)

Page 72: Crabs' eyes (*Proceedings of the Zoological Society*, 1907)

Page 73: *A Poodle* (1649) by Wenceslas Hollar (1607–1677). Available under Creative Commons Attribution/Share-A-Like Licence

Page 74: 'Head of the Flea' by William Lens Aldous (1792–1878) (*Entomological Society of London*, c.1838). Available under Creative Commons Attribution/Share-A-Like Licence

Page 75: *Otodectes* ear mite. By permission of Alan Walker, 2012. Available under Creative Commons Attribution/Share-A-Like Licence

Page 76: Beetle antennae from the *Descriptive Catalogue of the Coleoptera of South Africa* (1897) by Louis Péringuey (1855-1924). Available under Creative Commons Attribution/Share-A-Like Licence

Page 77: *Vespula vulgaris* under a scanning electron microscope by Secret Disc, 2007. Available under Creative Commons Attribution/Share-A-Like Licence

Page 78: Face of a southern yellow jacket queen (*Vespula squamosa*). By permission of Opo Terser, 2009. Available under Creative Commons Attribution/Share-A-Like Licence

Page 79: Face of a wolf spider. By permission of Opo Terser, 2008. Available under Creative Commons Attribution/Share-A-Like Licence

Page 80: From *Magnes sive de arte magnetica opus tripartitum* (1641) by Athanasius Kircher (c.1601–1680). Available under Creative Commons Attribution/Share-A-Like Licence

Page 81: *Mygale blondii* (*Popular Science Monthly*, 1881)

Page 82: Internal anatomy of the female two-lunged spider from *The Spider Book* (1912) by John Henry Comstock (1849–1931). Available under Creative Commons Attribution/Share-A-Like Licence

Page 83: Face of a wolf spider. By permission of Thomas Shahan, 2010. Available under Creative Commons Attribution/Share-A-Like Licence

Page 86: *Traité complet de l'anatomie de l'homme* (1862) by Nicolas-Henri Jacob (1782–1871) and Jean-Baptiste Bourgery (1797–1849). Available under Creative Commons Attribution/Share-A-Like Licence

Page 87: Muscles (*The Harmsworth Encyclopedia: Everybody's Book of Reference*, c.1905)

Page 88: Human compared to a factory (*The World of Wonder*, 1933)

Page 89: *Gray's Anatomy of the Human Body* (1918) by Henry Gray (1827–1861)

Page 90: 'Eat Your Soup': A baby and bib from a French catalogue c.1890. Available under Creative Commons Attribution/Share-A-Like Licence

Page 91: *Gray's Anatomy of the Human Body* (1918) by Henry Gray (1827–1861)

Page 92: *Gray's Anatomy of the Human Body* (1918) by Henry Gray (1827–1861)

Page 93: The mouths of lampreys (*Proceedings of the Zoological Society of London*, 1851)

Page 94: Radula (snail teeth) (Richard S. Houbrick, *Smithsonian Contributions to Zoology*, 1979)

Page 95: Scanning electron micrograph images of assorted love darts from Joris M. Koene and Hinrich Schulenberg, 'Shooting darts: co-evolution and counter-adaptation in hermaphroditic snails' (*BMC Evolutionary Biology*, 2005)

Page 96: Thaumatichthys (*Proceedings of the United States National Museum*, 1917). Courtesy of the Smithsonian Institution Libraries, Washington, D.C.

Page 97: Anglerfish, also known as the monkfish, *Lophius piscatorius* (*Popular Science Monthly*, 1879)

Page 98: Anatomy of a splendid alfonsino from *Collins Guide to the Sea Fishes of New Zealand* (1982) by Tony Ayling and Geoffrey Cox. Available under Creative Commons Attribution/Share-A-Like Licence

Page 99: From 'Mammalia, Aves, Reptilia, Amphibia, Pisces' (1909) by P. Matschie, A. Reichenow, G. Tornier, and P. Pappenheim, in A. Brauer, *Die Süsswasserfauna Deutschlands*. Available under Creative Commons Attribution/Share-A-Like Licence

Page 100: *Big Fish Eat Little Fish* (1556) by Pieter Breugel the Elder (c.1526/1530–1569). Available under Creative Commons Attribution/Share-A-Like Licence

Page 101: Hydra from *Locupletissimi Rerum Naturalium Thesauri*, Vol. 1 (1734) by Albertus Seba (1665–1736). Available under Creative Commons Attribution/Share-A-Like Licence

Page 102: *Portrait of Young Woman with Unicorn* (c.1505) by Raphael (1483–1520). Courtesy of the Soprintendenza Speciale per il Patrimonio Storico, Artistico ed Etnoantropologico e per il Polo Museale della citta di Roma

Page 102: *Cactus Man* (1881) by Odilon Redon (1840–1916). Available under Creative Commons Attribution/Share-A-Like Licence

Page 103: Illustration by Henry Holiday (1839–1927) for *The Hunting of the Snark* (1876). Available under Creative Commons Attribution/Share-A-Like Licence

Page 103: Centipede (*Popular Natural History*, 1923)

Page 104: *Cyrtoidea* from *Kunstformen der Natur* (1904) by Ernst Haeckel (1834–1919). Available under Creative Commons Attribution/Share-A-Like Licence

Page 108: Normal anatomy of the human eye and orbit, anterior view. By permission of Patrick J. Lynch, 2006. Available under Creative Commons Attribution Licence

Page 109: Visual portion of the retina as seen by ophthalmoscope (*Popular Science Monthly*, 1894)

Page 112: *Iris missouriensis* from *An Illustrated Flora of the Northern United States, Canada and the British Possessions* (1913) by Nathaniel Lord Britton and Addison Brown. Available under Creative Commons Attribution/Share-A-Like Licence

Page 113: Starlet (*The World of Wonder*, 1933)

Page 114: Iris by Thomas Piroli (1752–1824) from John Flaxman's *Iliad of Homer* (1795). Available under Creative Commons Attribution/Share-A-Like Licence

Page 115: *Gray's Anatomy of the Human Body* (1918) by Henry Gray (1827–1861). Copyright Elsevier

Page 115: *Demodex folliculorum* (*Popular Science Monthly*, 1878–1879)

Page 116: The eye of a fruit fly magnified under a scanning electron microscope. By permission of Louisa Howard, 2008. Available under Creative Commons Attribution/Share-A-Like Licence

Page 117: The wonder of the blind spot in the eye (*The World of Wonder*, 1933)

Page 118: Postcard by H. & C. H. London (no date), author's collection

Page 119: The Delboeuf illusion: both black circles are the same size

Page 120: A star with 1024 points. By permission of Mifter, 2008. Available under Creative Commons Attribution/Share-A-Like Licence

Page 120: A star with 100 points. By permission of Mifter, 2008. Available under Creative Commons Attribution/Share-A-Like Licence

Page 121: A tessellation of triangles. By permission of T. E. Dorczinski, 2010. Available under Creative Commons Attribution Licence

Page 122: An abyss of dodecagons. By permission of Baelde, 2012. Available under Creative Commons Attribution/Share-A-Like Licence

Page 123: Mandelbulb fractal of the North Pole. By permission of Ondrej Karlik, 2011. Available under Creative Commons Attribution/Share-A-Like Licence

Page 124: A Fraser spiral illusion. By permission of Mysid, 2007. Available under Creative Commons Attribution/Share-A-Like Licence

Page 125: The Ehrenstein illusion

Page 126: Gestalt illusions. By permission of Gestalt7. Available under Creative Commons Attribution/Share-A-Like Licence

Page 127: Satellite image of Lake Palanskoye, Kamchatka. By permission of NASA, 2012. Available under Creative Commons Attribution/Share-A-Like Licence

Page 128: Autostereogram. By permission of Martin Hawlisch, 2003. Available under Creative Commons Attribution/Share-A-Like Licence

Page 130: Gustav Fechner. Available under Creative Commons Attribution/Share-A-Like Licence

Page 130: Spinning disc (*Popular Science Monthly*, 1890–1891)

Page 131: The Fechner disc

Page 132: Hermann von Helmholtz (*Popular Science Monthly*, 1907)

Page 133: The Helmholtz disc

Page 134: Benham's artificial spectrum top

Page 135: Charles Benham (*Alma Mater Colcestriensis*, 1916)

Page 138: Adapted from work by Donald McGill c.1906

Page 142: The strange shadows on the wall (*The World of Wonder*, 1933)

Page 143: Illustration by J. J. Grandville (1803–1847) for *The Fables of Florian* (1842). Available under Creative Commons Attribution/Share-A-Like Licence

Page 145: Ghost-faced bat from *Kunstformen der Natur* (1904) by Ernst Haeckel (1834–1919). Available under Creative Commons Attribution/Share-A-Like Licence

Page 148: *Mercury* (date unknown) by Wenceslas Hollar (1607–1677). Available under Creative Commons Attribution/Share-A-Like Licence

Page 149: Greek postage stamp (1861). Available under Creative Commons Attribution/Share-A-Like Licence

Page 153: Specimens of trade charms (*Folk-Lore: A Quarterly Review of Myth, Tradition, Institution & Customs*, 1902). Available under Creative Commons Attribution/Share-A-Like Licence